Ladybird
by Design

Ladybird
by Design

Lawrence Zeegen

LADYBIRD BOOKS

UK | USA | Canada | Ireland | Australia
India | New Zealand | South Africa

Ladybird Books is part of the Penguin Random House group
of companies whose addresses can be found at
global.penguinrandomhouse.com.

ladybird.com

Penguin
Random House
UK

First published 2015

001

Set in Adobe Sabon, Gill Sans and Ladybird 563 Brand
Interiors designed by Tom Sanderson
Cover designed by Ladybird Books Ltd
Project editor: Emma Marriott

Printed in China

A CIP catalogue record for this book is available from the British Library

ISBN: 978–0–723–29392–7

Contents

Ladybird by Design

Introduction
From publishing sideline to national treasure

For generations of British children Ladybird books occupied a very special place in their young lives. A Ladybird book offered a utopian vision of an innocent world – where learning to read was fun, nursery rhymes were enchanting, nature was abundant, history was heroic, science was enthralling and modern life was seemingly bathed in the bright sunshine of an eternal summer.

In today's fast-paced, twenty-four/seven, 360-degree global village, it can be challenging to remember a Britain that shut down at 5 p. m., with early closing on Wednesdays and all-day closing on Sundays. The Ladybird world of the 1950s, 1960s and 1970s was a safe and simple one; a world where Mummy shopped at the greengrocer's on the high street and cooked delicious meals in the kitchen, whilst children played catch in the garden and Daddy washed his car on the drive.

Ladybird books covered every possible subject and interest, published across a vast array of series. From Key Words, Learning to Read, Well-loved Tales, Nature, Animal Stories and Bible Stories to Adventures from History, Sport and Achievements, Hobbies and Interests, People at Work and How it Works, there wasn't a topic or theme left untouched by Ladybird's guiding hand.

The Ladybird tone of voice was authoritative, but never condescending. Ladybird language was open and honest, nurturing and caring, down-to-earth, yet also aspirational. Quintessentially British, but with truly global appeal, Ladybird was a trusted British brand akin to the BBC, Rolls-Royce and Marks & Spencer.

The success of Ladybird books was as much due to a clever format and compelling design as it was to the quality of the writing and the strong editorial stance. Pocket-sized and collectible, Ladybird books presented an enchanting portrait of their time through specially commissioned artwork, unparalleled in its perfectly observed attention to detail and sense of place. Ladybird's full-colour, full-page illustrations, often created by well-known illustrators, such as Charles Tunnicliffe and Allen W. Seaby, were the window into the Ladybird world. Ladybird books were a precise marriage of style and content, the design providing a perfect framework for straightforward and honest editorial content.

In truth, the successful format was born more of necessity than by design. Books carrying the Ladybird logo were first produced in 1915 by Wills & Hepworth, a commercial printing company in Loughborough, near Leicester, who decided to use the time between jobs, when their presses were otherwise idle, to publish inexpensive children's books. It wasn't, however, until after the start of the Second World War that Wills & Hepworth came up with its iconic format as a result of paper shortages: a book of fifty-six pages printed in full-colour from a single sheet of 40-inch by 30-inch paper – the optimum and most economical size for the printing presses in Loughborough.

For 100 years, Ladybird Books Ltd, a very British publishing phenomenon, has delighted children and their parents and teachers alike, taking readers through a journey of discovery and enlightenment. Accessible and affordable – the hardbacks were sold at 2/6d, (half a crown) from 1940 up until decimalization in the 1970s – the books could be purchased in newsagents and toy shops as well as book shops. By the early 1970s, Ladybird books were being published in over thirty languages, making a significant impact on generations of young readers around the world as well as in the UK.

For so many, a new Ladybird book represented the beginning of things – a new interest or hobby, a thirst for scientific discovery, a connection with nature or a bond with an historical figure. Most important of all, a new Ladybird book represented a rite of passage – a sense of independence from parent and teacher and a quest to embrace knowledge on one's own terms, in one's own time.

Now undeniably considered a national treasure, Ladybird Books has a place in the nation's psyche; our collective memories hold dear the influence of these charming books. A Ladybird book evokes strong feelings; deep-rooted

PAGE 2:
Ladybird advertisement from the 1950s. Note that the price of Ladybird books here is 3s. Wills & Hepworth briefly experimented with a price increase during this period before going back to 2/6d.

PREVIOUS PAGE:
Shopping with Mother
563 Learning to Read, 1958.
Illustrations by J. H. Wingfield.

Ladybird by Design

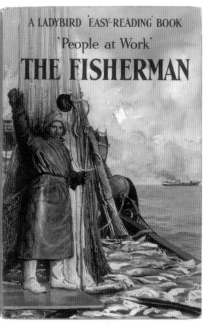

2c *I Like to Write*
641 Key Words, 1965.
Illustrations by Martin Aitchison.

The Fisherman
606B People at Work,
1963. Illustrations by John Berry.

Cinderella
606D Well-loved Tales,
1964. Illustrations by Eric Winter.

What to Look for in Summer
536 Nature, 1960.
Illustrations by C. F. Tunnicliffe.

11c Books are Exciting
641 Key Words, 1967.
Illustrations by
Martin Aitchison.

Ladybird by Design

memories of a time and a place when a simply designed and cheaply produced book could resonate across generations of readers. Ladybird represents an era before the rise of the PC and the Internet, before smartphones and tablets, before computer games and social media.

Ladybird by Design investigates the cultural significance and social impact of these little books, exploring their editorial and production origins, their design, the aesthetics of their typography and illustration, and the unique way in which they captured a very British childhood. It delves into the lushly illustrated utopian world of Ladybird, unpacking the emotional, cultural and iconic power of a unique slice of Britain's visual history.

Ladybird newspaper advertisement, 1960s.

W. W. R.
P. W. R.
J. S. CLEGG, A.C.A.
J. BROOMER
J. B. ROBERTS

PWORTH LTD

OF LADYBIRD CHILDREN'S BOOKS

S • LOUGHBOROUGH

12th October 1949.

Lithographic and letterpress colour printe

The Angel Press
LOUGHBOROUGH

Telephone: Loughborough 2502 • Telegrams: W

I. The Origin of the Species

D.H.Keen, Esq.,
    c/o Marigolds,
      Manor Road
      Stratford on Avon.

Dear Keen,

    I have very much pleasure
you that the directors have again th
the payment of bonuses and in this c
enclosing a cheque which is made out
after the deduction of P.A.Y.E. Inco
certificate in this connection is al

    The war is going very well
to have you back again as soon as po
interested to have your demobilizati
some future date circumstances arise
could be of any help in getting your
know and I will do my best to assist

    Very best wishes.

        Yours

your reminder regarding informat
e are sending out this week advi
ney and I will endeavour to writ
n next Friday week, the 21st, wi
entral London calls and with par
Times Exhibition.

r your note regarding Lewis's.
selling many more Ladybird Bool
proper buyer, Mr. Williams who
the present time, about 6-month
anwhile, the buying is being dor
or their Libraries, who has par
ate the sales that could be effe
Display Material, etc.

    Yours sincerely,

      Wills & Hepworth I

JSC/KMF.

worth Ltd.

nd Advertising Agents

DIRECTORS
W. S. HEPWORTH
P. W. ROBERTS
J. S. CLEGG, A.C.A.

& Hepworth, Loughborough

29th March 1945

riting to advise
year arranged for
ction I am
the net sum
ax. The necessary
nclosed.

we are very anxious
le. I should be
umber and if at
ereby you think I
ease then let me

rely,

ILLS & HEPWORTH LTD

OLOUR PRINTERS AND ADVERTISING AGENTS

E ANGEL PRESS • LOUGHBOROUGH • Leicestershire

WPJJHDA
L

BY GIVEN that the thirtyseventh Annual General
will be held at the Offices of the Company,
ghborough, on Tuesday the eighteenth day of Ju

for the purpose of transacting the following

e Statement of Accounts
61, and to consider tl
rts thereon.

itors for the ensuing

h other business of
cted at an Ordinary

port of the Directo

any are sent herew

d to attend and

a proxy to atte

be a member of

By order

M.

Sec
y of June t

The Shie
Sandispl
Maide
1st, Ma

Dear Mr. Keen,

If you are agreeable I i
to propose you as a Director o
Company at our meeting on the
instant.

Mr. Clegg will notify you i
it is carried after that date.

Yours sincerely,

Hepworth

The open-winged Ladybird logo was first registered in 1915 and, though it would be updated during the course of its hundred-year lifespan, it was that first design which provided the DNA for what would become an iconic brand.

The Wills & Hepworth offices in Loughborough.

Wills's Almanac, an early example of Wills & Hepworth printing, 1890.

PREVIOUS PAGE:
Wills & Hepworth
correspondence, 1940s.

Wills & Hepworth Limited
The history of the company

It would be easy to describe the origins of Ladybird as a series of happy accidents, when it was actually also the result of shrewd business prowess. The company's humble beginnings in Loughborough belie the huge impact that Ladybird books have had on young readers across many decades or the company's vast influence on children's publishing in Britain and around the world.

In 1867, Henry Wills, a businessman in Loughborough, opened a bookshop in the marketplace before branching out into running a lending library, selling newspapers and magazines, supplying office stationery and, for a short time, working as a travel agent. Expanding his business into printing after the acquisition of new premises, Wills began publishing the *Wills's Loughborough Almanac, Trade Guide and Street Directory* and printing under contract the *Loughborough Echo* newspaper.

William Hepworth, another local businessman with printing experience and a long-time friend of Henry Wills, became a partner in the business in 1904 and Wills & Hepworth Limited was born. Whilst the name Wills & Hepworth survived for decades, the partnership was short-lived: Henry Wills retired and sold his share of the business in 1905, just a year after the formation of the company.

In 1914, it was William Hepworth who made the bold but ultimately wise decision to establish and launch his own range of children's books. He took this step at a critical time. The outbreak of the First World War had led to a restriction in book production due to the scarcity of paper and other raw

Ladybird by Design

The original open-winged
Ladybird logo, first registered
in 1915.

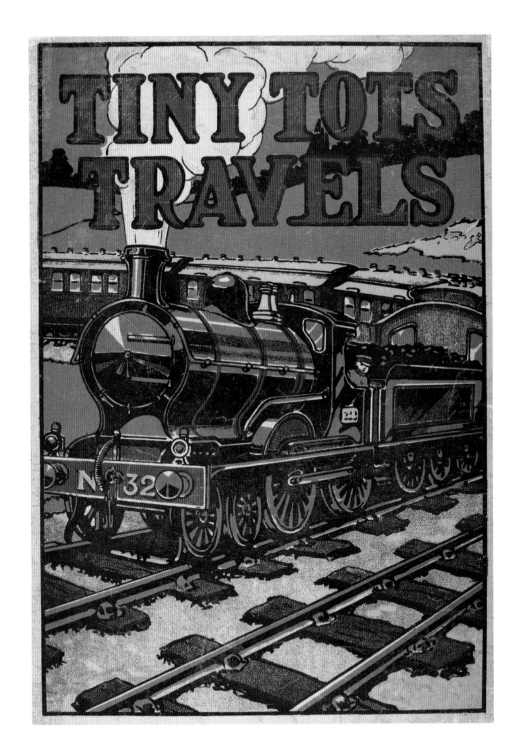

materials, but demand for literature, and in particular children's literature, was high.

Hepworth's entry into the world of children's publishing was taken with small and cautious steps. He published just two titles in 1914 and each featured black ink line drawings both as full-page illustrations and integrated into the text. The full-colour board cover of *Tiny Tots Travels* shows a brightly coloured steam train, whilst *Hans Andersen's Fairy Tales* depicts a young girl watching the flight of crowned geese over the sea.

Later titles also had the accompanying phrase 'The Ladybird Series' on the front covers. The open-winged Ladybird logo was first registered in 1915 and, though it would be updated during the course of its hundred-year lifespan, it was that first design which provided the DNA for what would become an iconic brand.

Between publication of the first Ladybird titles and the outbreak of the Second World War in 1939, production of children's books was erratic. Utilizing dead machine time – when the presses weren't producing numerous large-scale, full-colour catalogues for car manufacturers Austin and Rover, motorcycle manufacturer BSA, and perfume-makers Yardley – Wills & Hepworth's Ladybird books remained a low-risk and rather miniscule sideline to their core business.

Hans Andersen's Fairy Tales
*c.*1914.
Illustrator unknown.

OPPOSITE PAGE:
Tiny Tots Travels
*c.*1914.
Illustrator unknown.

THE ROVER 2-LITRE 60

THE ROVER 75

BOTH PAGES:
Some examples of full-colour catalogues printed by Wills & Hepworth from the 1930s to 1950s.

Ladybird by Design

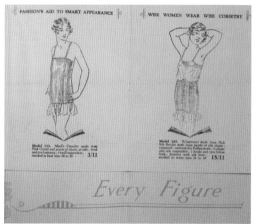

The First Ladybird Titles

Wills & Hepworth's early foray into the children's book market was varied. The design and production techniques employed differed from publication to publication, with the publishers freely utilizing a variety of formats, printing on to different paper stocks and using several binding techniques. The firm's output spanned the entire spectrum – from the very cheapest of books printed on poor-quality paper and sold to market hucksters to substantial volumes with full-colour illustrations, lavish end-papers, decorated spines and printed on high quality paper. Wills & Hepworth, with no consistent house style, was clearly testing every market.

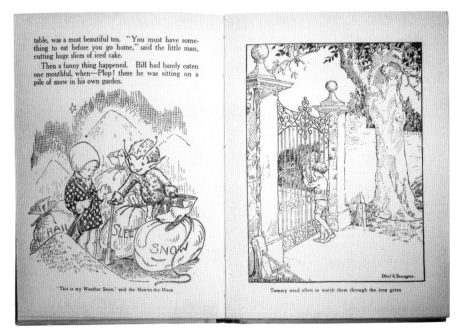

table, was a most beautiful tea. "You must have something to eat before you go home," said the little man, cutting huge slices of iced cake.

Then a funny thing happened. Bill had barely eaten one mouthful, when—Plop! there he was sitting on a pile of snow in his own garden.

"This is my Weather Store," said the Man-in-the-Moon

Tommy used often to watch them through the iron gates

TALES OF THE TRAIN

OF THE

TRAIN

NO 15

THE LADYBIRD SERIES

1. The Origin of the Species

21

A Trip on the Sea
*c.*1915.
Illustrator unknown.

Tales of Ships & Trains
*c.*1915.
Illustrator unknown.

Billy and the Treasure
*c.*1915.
Illustrator unknown.

Little Sports
*c.*1915.
Illustrator unknown.

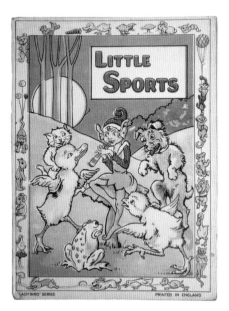

Ladybird by Design

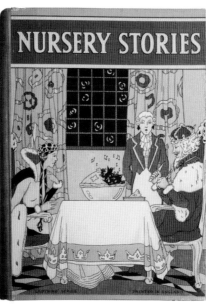

Old Nursery Rhymes
c. 1915.
Illustrator unknown.

Nursery Stories
c. 1915.
Illustrator unknown.

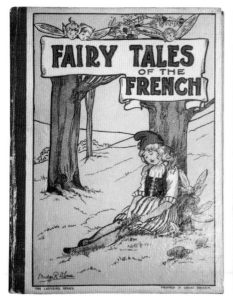

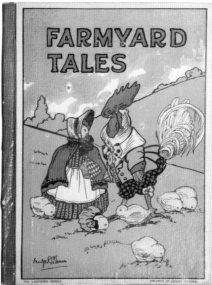

Fairy Tales of the French
*c.*1915.
Illustrator unknown.

Farmyard Tales
*c.*1915.
Illustrator unknown.

Form Follows Function
Early production decisions and resulting design choices

Second World War
paper-rationing poster.

An example of wartime
paper rationing.

Ladybird's Managing Director,
James Shields Clegg, and his
wife Sylvia at their home
in Loughborough.

The introduction of a standard Ladybird format was clearly influenced by the necessities of production, although it was also enhanced by astute design thinking. The decision to adopt a consistent format could be attributed to a very British proverb: 'necessity is the mother of invention'. As likely a justification, however, may well have been the design mantra: 'form follows function'.

For Wills & Hepworth, the 1939 outbreak of war and the impending rationing of paper was the kick-start the company needed to rethink the design and production of their Ladybird titles. With the import of all goods severely restricted, in February 1940 the British government limited publishers to sixty per cent of their pre-war paper consumption and then again to forty per cent in December 1941.

Forced to reduce their print runs, publishers began to look at how best to utilize the limited paper available to them. Narrower margins and smaller type sizes increased the amount of content on each page, and thinner paper stocks enabled greater use of a resource governed by weight. The 1942 Book Production War Economy Agreement, initiated by The Publishers Association, began to prescribe the weight and quality of paper and the width of margins, as well as permissible type sizes and even the number of words per inch – restrictions that would radically impact book design and production. Fortunately for Wills & Hepworth, the agreement would not affect illustrated books or titles aimed at children under the age of eleven years. Whilst not enforced by regulatory control, Ladybird's redesign of its format was however clearly influenced by the wartime situation, with rationing now part of the national psyche.

James Shields Clegg, having joined the company in 1934 as an accountant and en route to his eventual role as managing director, was given the task of combating potential shortages of paper. He and the Wills & Hepworth print and production team began work on devising a new format, which would unwittingly take Wills & Hepworth to the forefront of children's publishing.

The solution to the problem of paper shortage was to minimize wastage. Beginning from the premise that the largest sheet of paper available to the publishers measured 40 inches by 30 inches, it made sense to create a book that utilized every bit of the paper. From this, the Wills & Hepworth team

Ladybird by Design

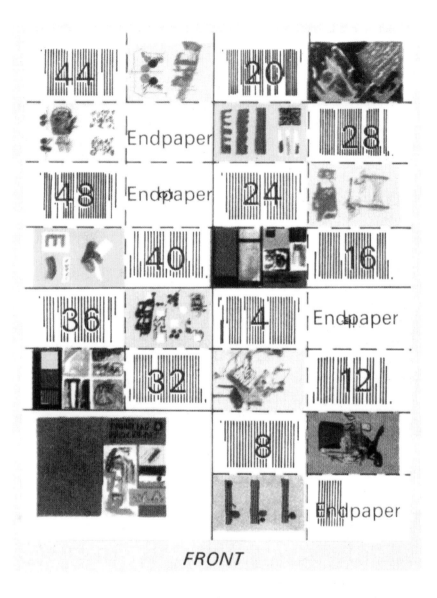

An example of how a
Ladybird book was printed.
Fifty-six pages, including cover
and end-papers, were printed
on to both sides of a single piece
of paper measuring 40 inches
by 30 inches, then cut, folded
and bound. This is the front side.
Taken from
Printing Processes
654 How it Works, 1971.
Illustrations by B. H. Robinson.

FRONT

The reverse side
of a single-sheet printing.
Taken from
Printing Processes
654 How it Works, 1971.
Illustrations by B. H. Robinson.

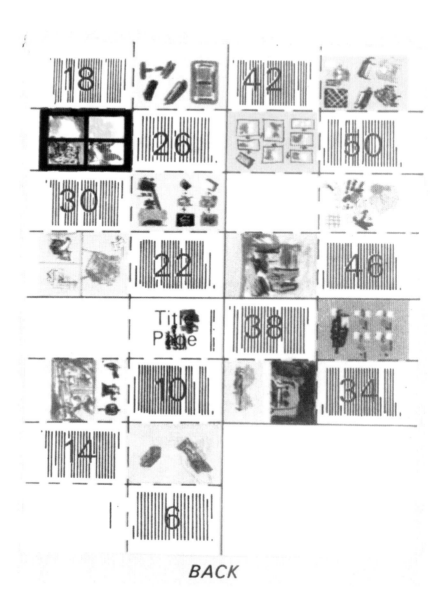

BACK

Ladybird by Design

devised the format of a 56-page book, with each page measuring 7 inches by 4 5/8 inches, and all of which could be printed from a single sheet of paper along with the end-papers and dust jacket.

The new Ladybird format allowed for a full-colour illustration on every recto (right-hand) page, with corresponding text on the verso (left-hand) page. The books featured plenty of white space, generous line spacing and an accessible font size – perfectly aligned with the age range the books were intended for. With production set up so it could be easily automated, the one-size-fits-all format enabled books to be produced efficiently and cheaply. The printing presses could run unhindered, producing large volumes at low cost. This became vital to the success of Ladybird.

An example of a folded single sheet from *Tootles the Taxi*.

BUNNIKIN'S PICNIC PARTY

Bunnikin's Picnic Party
401 Animal Stories Told in Verse,
1940. Illustrations by
A. J. MacGregor.

Bunnikin's Picnic Party

Wills & Hepworth's new single-sheet format created a book perfectly sized for the hands of young children. The first book published in this new small hardback format was *Bunnikin's Picnic Party* in 1940. It told the story of a rabbit's day out at a picnic, written in verse by W. Perring and illustrated by Anguisine Jeanne MacGregor. The book's colourful illustrations and simple rhyming story were popular with pre-school children and it became the first title in Animal Stories Told in Verse (series 401). Two new titles followed in the same year – *The First Day of the Holidays* and *Ginger's Adventures* – with another three titles the next year: *Smoke and Fluff*, *Jeremy's Day in the Country* and *Bob Bushtail's Adventure*.

Bunnikin's Picnic Party
401 Animal Stories Told in Verse,
1940. Illustrations by
A. J. MacGregor.

Sure enough, he followed quickly,
   Till they found a pleasant glade;
Fluff unpacked the laden baskets,
   Laid the teacloth in the shade.

Set out all the cups and saucers,
   Put the cakes upon a plate:
At the tempting sight the others,
   Gath'ring wood, could scarcely wait.

BOTH PAGES:
Production images from Wills & Hepworth
from the 1900s to the 1970s.

Becoming a National Treasure
A change of direction

Douglas Keen in the 1930s. Keen first started working for Wills & Hepworth Ltd around this time. In this image he is modelling a suit for a Birmingham tailor.

Douglas Keen, the WHSmith head buyer and James Shields Clegg at a book fair, 1960s.

OPPOSITE PAGE:
A Book of Birds & Eggs prototype book cover, 1952.

Ownership of one's very first Ladybird book was undoubtedly a rite of passage. Whether you were given one for a birthday or Christmas gift, bought it for 2/6d out of your hard-earned pocket money, or won one as a school prize, owning a Ladybird book was a distinctly enriching experience.

Your first Ladybird book marked the beginning of a journey that could see you enter the magical world of a story, connect with figures from history, study a species of flower or bird, grapple with science, gain new geographic knowledge, acquire new hobbies, interests and practical skills, or understand the vast complexities of the wider world around you.

Ladybird understood how to present the world to a young audience through words and pictures, and how vital it was to communicate visual and literary clarity with just the right tone of voice. For any child buying, being given, borrowing or winning a Ladybird book, here was the start of their own personal association with new and known knowledge through well-written, well-designed and well-edited content.

Just as the perfect marriage of form and function had come together to create the 56-page single-sheet format, so too was the vital connection made between words and images and their importance in balancing education and entertainment. Again, this was no happy accident or fortuitous pathway, but instead the sheer determination of a Wills & Hepworth employee.

Douglas Keen understood the child audience, and had the vision to move the company from publishing glossy commercial brochures to children's books, inadvertently beginning a revolution in children's publishing.

Having first joined the company as a travelling salesman in 1936, Keen returned after serving in the Second World War and began a crusade to convince the directors to continue publishing Ladybird books. Wills & Hepworth's intention had been to revert back to printing car brochures as soon as the war ended, ceasing production of all children's books. The success of James Clegg's new single-sheet format along with growing sales, however, enabled Keen to change the directors' minds. As a result, the company continued publishing Ladybird books throughout the remainder of the 1940s, keeping to the proven formula of books for young children primarily based on fairy tales and stories about animals.

A Book of
BIRDS & EGGS
in colour

Douglas Keen and his wife Margaret in the 1940s.

Keen, however, was increasingly set on expanding Ladybird's reach and remit by branching out into educational titles. He researched the market thoroughly, travelling to shops and schools across Britain to gather information about what children liked, responded to and read. Despite an initially negative response to his ideas in 1948, Keen remained undeterred and set about creating a prototype book to support his rationale.

Working with his wife Margaret and mother-in-law Margaret Jones, both trained artists, Keen compiled a makeshift dummy book entitled *A Book of Birds & Eggs*. It combined factual knowledge written in an easy-to-read style but with an authoritative tone of voice and sensitively illustrated images – part artistic interpretation and part natural history. Keen had a lifelong passion for the natural world, which must have influenced his choice of subject matter, and he was also astutely aware of the lack of appropriate, fully illustrated bird books for enthusiasts.

Keen's approach paid off; the directors were convinced and Keen's dummy was used as the format for *British Birds and their Nests*, which was published in 1953 and became the first title in Ladybird's new Nature series (536).

Keen could never have envisaged quite what a dramatic impact his ideas would have on the fortunes of Ladybird – sales of 24,000 of the standardized format in 1946 grew to in excess of 24 million by 1974 when he retired. The rite of passage enjoyed by Ladybird's young readers was no longer limited to the lucky few; success, expansion and market leadership now ensured every British child could gain access to the world of Ladybird at home, in the classroom and in libraries up and down the country.

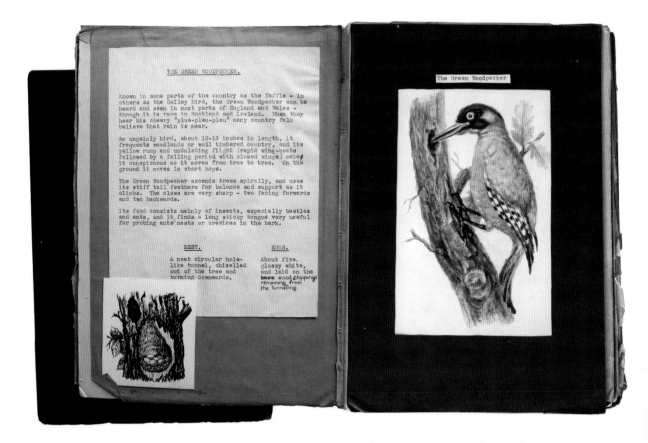

A Design Prototype

Design was to play a key role in helping establish the direction that
Ladybird would take. Douglas Keen understood the importance of the
design prototype and how a physical artefact could showcase his vision for
Wills & Hepworth's Ladybird books.

It was likely that Keen's previous training as a sign-writer in advertising
played a vital part in his understanding of the importance of concise
wording, grammatical accuracy and careful proofreading. Equally likely are
the lessons he learned in advertising about the effectiveness of showing a
client a mock-up during a presentation. This knowledge of and interest in
lettering, typography and design influenced the appearance of Ladybird
books throughout his working life.

A Book of Birds & Eggs
prototype interior spread, 1952.

THE GREAT-TIT.

Known as the "Saw-Sharpener" because its call "Teacher, Teacher" sounds like the sharpening of a saw, this active bird has similar habits and frequents the same spots as the Blue-Tit. There is, however, a considerable difference in appearance, for the crown of his head is blue-black - as are his chin, throat and a band which runs down the centre of his breast.

Do not confuse this bird with the Coal-Tit, which, although it has a head similar to that of the Great-Tit, is a smaller, duller bird, is buff and not yellow underneath, and - most noticeable features of all - has a large white patch on its nape and no dark band down its breast.

NEST.	EGGS.
The nest of the Great Tit may be in similar spots to that of the Blue-Tit, constructed with the same materials.	Seven to eleven in number. Colour and markings as in other Tits.

Ladybird by Design

The Great Tit

A Book of Birds & Eggs
prototype interior spread, 1952.

Ladybird Window Displays

Much of the early success of Ladybird books was due to the presentation of the brand and the marketing of the books, with the Ladybird message reaching its target audiences of children, parents and teachers. Douglas Keen recognized that the brand had to be prominent in retail outlets and ensured that this would occur by design and not by happenstance.

Post-war shops in Britain were still rather dowdy in presentation; the glitz and glare that typified the marketing of goods by their US counterparts had yet to be adopted in the UK. This hadn't gone unnoticed by Keen – he set about commissioning local carpenters to build display units for Ladybird books and, working with a sign-writer, he crafted colourful shelving units and cabinets that could be erected on-site. Much of this he would deliver personally in his car, bringing Ladybird books to prominence in book shops and toy stores. Many of the items used in the displays were made at Keen's home in Stratford-Upon-Avon, with input from his wife and mother-in-law.

BOTH PAGES:
A selection of Ladybird window displays from the 1940s and 1950s.

Ladybird by Design

BOTH PAGES:
A selection of Ladybird book
displays from the 1940s and 1950s.

Ladybird by Design

The Innocent Ladybird World
Childhood captured through words and pictures

Jenny, one of Douglas Keen's daughters, *c.*1950 – one of many children who enjoyed reading Ladybird books.

One aspect of Ladybird's success was the close affinity it had with its young readership. These were books that appealed on so many levels to children and their parents, grandparents and teachers – the wholesome goodness of Ladybird and the warm feelings that the books evoked were unmatched by children's books published elsewhere.

A combination of factors created the complete childhood compendium: Ladybird's use of design and illustration, chiming so well with the optimistic sense of a utopian future, paired with authoritative language exploring every facet of entertainment and knowledge.

The expertly crafted bespoke illustrations within each book were executed by many of the top commercial artists and illustrators of their day. It was the attention to detail in the illustrations – the nuanced sense of realism, the portrayal of believable characters in believable settings living believable lives – coupled with an approachable editorial style that captured the imagination and interest of the reader. Despite the very British perspective and the uncompromisingly optimistic view of the world, here was a visual and written language that resonated with children.

Whether a factual or fictional title, the Ladybird tone of voice was clearly present – trustworthy, dependable and respected. Just as children's programming on BBC radio and television was thought of as morally correct, honourable and upright, so too was Ladybird's stance in children's publishing. Young readers could identify with the world portrayed by Ladybird and, whilst it may not have accurately reflected their own, they could project their ambitions towards the seemingly perfect lives of its characters, such as the Key Words protagonists Peter and Jane.

The goals and aspirations, rather than the everyday realities of post-war British children, were played out across numerous Ladybird series where the overriding sense was of taking pleasure in simple, natural things and a happy, well-ordered domesticity. An era of optimism and self-belief, fuelled by the jubilation of wartime victory, would permeate the Ladybird childhood.

1a *Play with us*
641 Key Words, 1964.
Illustrations by
J. H. Wingfield.

Text and Image

The design decision to
pair a single page of text
with an illustration or
collection of related images
on the opposite page of every
Ladybird book was brilliantly
simple yet effective. The
marriage of text and image
was perfectly balanced – each
page of text typographically
designed and ordered so that
it was utterly appropriate to
the age and reading ability
of the young audience.
Every illustrated image was
beautifully reproduced in
full colour and designed to
elucidate and complement
the written word.

6

Peter and Jane

1b Look at This
641 Key Words, 1964.
Illustrations by
J. H. Wingfield.

I. The Origin of the Species

II. A Design for Life

The key to a successful set of illustrations for a Ladybird title was in the attention to detail – parents and teachers grew to trust the reliability of the images, and the books acted as strong pictorial references for many subjects and disciplines.

A Design for Life

Ladybird books held a dear place in the hearts and minds of their young readership. The deep-rooted association with one's youth either through the eyes of Peter and Jane, via the enchanting world of a fairy tale or through the first glimpse into the working lives of adults is extremely evocative for generations of readers.

This unique place in people's affections, however, wasn't won easily; the status of national treasure wasn't to be dished out willy-nilly. Ladybird and Wills & Hepworth worked hard to earn this distinguished place in the nation's heart. The balance of finely executed texts – from Vera Southgate's skilled traditional storytelling in the Well-loved Tales series to the expertly researched work on the teaching of reading by William Murray and Joe McNally for the Key Words Reading Scheme – was critical to Ladybird's success. Ladybird books, whether grounded in fact or floating in fiction, were the first and last place for quality text, verse and prose for Britain's newest readers.

Alongside the well-crafted text, however, it was imperative that the design, layout and illustration of Ladybird books was also unparalleled. The work of the type-setters and illustrators was as important as that of the writers and no one understood this more acutely than the eventual editorial director, Douglas Keen. It was Keen who insisted that attention should be paid to the layout and illustrations. He commissioned the very best artists and illustrators and built strong working relationships – and often personal friendships – between artists and writers.

PREVIOUS PAGE:
The Computer
654 How it Works, 1971.
Original artwork by
B. H. Robinson.

7a Happy Holidays
641 Key Words, 1964.
Illustrations by J. H. Wingfield.

The key to a successful set of illustrations for a Ladybird title was in the attention to detail – parents and teachers grew to trust the reliability of the images and the books acted as strong pictorial references for many subjects and disciplines. The factual titles comprised illustrations that were true to life; they depicted a world that was real, complete and believable.

Often working from sourced and self-generated photographic references, as well as their own location drawings, the Ladybird illustrator was a professional artist of great talent, hand-picked for his or her ability to bring situations and settings to life. But Ladybird illustrations did much more than simply capture a moment or make the mundane memorable; they added something to the story. They frequently applied additional meaning to the text, layered further complexities to scenarios and gave young readers images that they could get lost in – Adventures from History (series 561) captured epic battle scenes with amazing fluidity, whilst Bible Stories (series 522) brought the tales of Christianity to life with real visual appeal.

The world of Ladybird, as created by numerous Ladybird illustrators and artists, was a visual one ready to be explored, with each of the twenty-four full-colour images of every title always beautifully crafted and expertly conceived.

The Little Lord Jesus
522 Bible Stories, 1954.
Illustrations by
Kenneth Inns.

Alexander the Great
561 Adventures from History,
1963. Illustrations
by John Kenney.

The Story of Joseph
522 Bible Stories, 1955.
Illustrations by Kenneth Inns.

Florence Nightingale
561 Adventures from History,
1959. Illustrations
by John Kenney.

The Little Lord Jesus
522 Bible Stories, 1954.
Illustrations by Kenneth Inns.

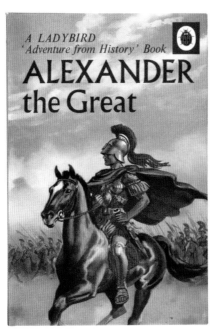

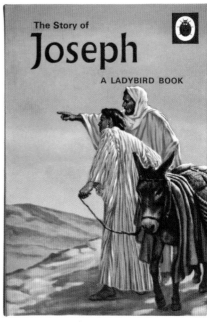

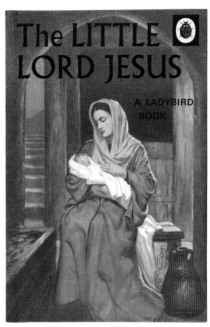

Ladybird by Design

Stories about Jesus the Helper
606A Easy Reading Bible Stories,
1960. Illustrations by
Clive Uptton.

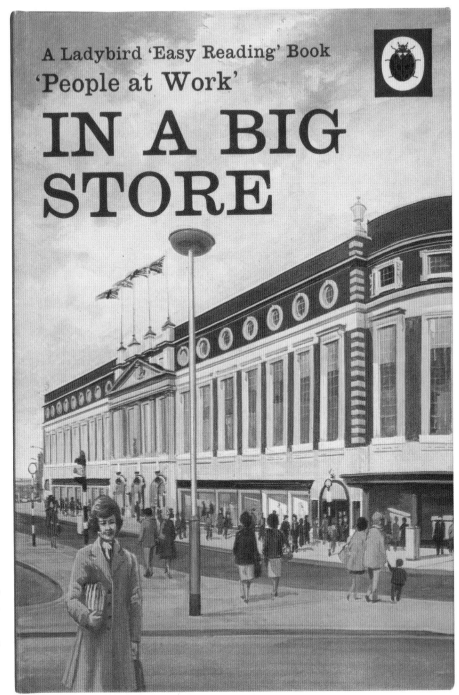

A Ladybird 'Easy Reading' Book

'People at Work'

IN A BIG STORE

The reference for this cover image is the Bentalls store in Kingston-upon-Thames.

In a Big Store
606B People at Work, 1973.
Illustrations by John Berry.

Ladybird by Design

Sometimes alterations have to be made to clothes bought by customers. The customer tries on the clothes and the assistant marks the correct measurements on them. She then takes the clothes to the sewing room where the alterations are made. Dresses, skirts or coats might have to be made shorter or longer. Some clothes might need adjustment to the seams to make them fit better.

There is always plenty of work on clothes or other articles for the girls and women who work in the sewing room.

28

In a Big Store
606B People at Work,
1973. Illustrations by John Berry.

Letters and telephone calls, from people who wish to book rooms, all go to the reception desk. The receptionist has charts which show her which rooms are empty. She knows all the rooms and tries to give people the sort of room they want. The receptionist tells the head housekeeper which rooms must be made ready for new guests each day, and which guests are leaving.

In smaller hotels there is a telephone switchboard at the reception desk. Incoming calls can be put through to guests' rooms and to all parts of the hotel. The receptionist can use a loudspeaker system to call guests if they are wanted. In large hotels there is a separate telephone exchange and operator.

8

In a Hotel
606B People at Work,
1972. Illustrations by John Berry.

Douglas Keen

A wartime photo of Douglas Keen, showing him in his RAF uniform.

Douglas Keen's family home in Stratford-upon-Avon. He designed it and had it built in the 1950s and his office, the 'editorial department of Wills & Hepworth', is the single-storey extension on the right-hand side.

Much of Ladybird's success in the period following the end of the Second World War can be attributed to the vision and dedication of one man: Douglas Keen. Keen was the driving force in turning Ladybird from a small independent company into the major global contender in children's books that it was to become.

Born into a working-class family in Cheltenham Spa in Gloucestershire, Keen's own childhood was unlike the one depicted in Ladybird books. His father, a market gardener, left the family home when Keen was a young boy and his mother supported the family single-handed by working as a home-based dress-maker and milliner. Keen won a scholarship to the prestigious Pate's Grammar School before then going on to study art and marketing at evening classes.

From an early age Keen was a true believer in the value and importance of education as a way out of poverty. His thirst for knowledge and belief in self-improvement were to become the basis for encouraging millions of children, through Ladybird books, to enjoy learning.

Keen joined Wills & Hepworth as a salesman in 1936, at the age of twenty-three. However, Keen's starring role in determining Ladybird's future came after he returned to Wills & Hepworth in 1946, following a six-year absence serving in the RAF as part of a mobile radar unit. He travelled the UK as a company rep, meeting and speaking with bookshop owners and teachers, and gathering a real sense of what sort of books British children wanted. Ladybird's move into printing and publishing books cheaply on a single sheet of paper hadn't been properly investigated and it was through conversations with teachers and shopkeepers that Keen observed a major gap in the market for well-researched and illustrated hardback factual books on interesting subjects.

Keen convinced the Wills & Hepworth board that his idea was worth pursuing through the creation of a prototype book about birds. He wrote the text, the illustrations were created by his mother-in-law, Margaret Jones, a trained artist, and the line drawings by his wife, also called Margaret.

After the board's approval of this new direction, Keen began work on series after series of Ladybird books. He was made a company director in March 1957, but, for many years afterwards,

Keen and his part-time secretary were the entire Ladybird editorial department.

Keen often held meetings in and commissioned authors and artists from his home office, an extension built on to the side of his house in Stratford-upon-Avon. Keen's relationship with those that he commissioned was vital – many of the illustrators worked for the publisher for many years because of their enduring friendship with Keen and his honest and meticulous approach to commissioning and planning.

Douglas Keen's lasting legacy at Ladybird may be measured by the huge success of the Key Words Reading Scheme, which taught generations of children to read, the People at Work and How it Works series, and the numerous books on nature or the many titles covering history. His impact on the education of British children between the late 1940s and the mid-1970s – the golden age of Ladybird – simply can not be overestimated.

Keen took early retirement in 1973 following the takeover of Ladybird by Pearson Longman, at a time when sales averaged 20 million copies per year. He died in 2008 aged ninety-five.

Douglas Keen in the 1970s. A colour version of this photograph was mounted on canvas and displayed in the boardroom in the Loughborough offices.

Keen and his wife Margaret in the mid-1970s. Margaret Keen was for a while also on the Ladybird payroll, contributing creative ideas for books as well as proof-reading titles.

A Social History of Utopian Modernism

Formica and Stag brochures promoting ultra-modern furniture and homewares. Published by Wills & Hepworth in the 1960s.

If the foundation stones for Ladybird's success were laid during the post-war years, it was the 1960s that really saw the publishing company go from strength to strength. The 1960s saw the post-war baby boomers come of age, creating a mass of new consumers who were open and optimistic, confident and unrestrained. Britain was finally out of the bleak austerity that had followed the end of the Second World War and this army of new and willing customers eagerly embraced change.

Ladybird was keen to grasp hold of this new modernism, albeit primarily in terms of design, fashion and architecture, as depicted in its illustrations during the 1960s. Whilst the Key Words nuclear family of Mummy, Daddy, Peter and Jane represented conventional family values – there were no single-parent or mixed-race families – Ladybird's visuals appealed to a forward-looking, if not necessarily forward-thinking, modernist.

Modernism was about the here and now and new aspirations. Out went the fusty bygone era of past generations, of scrimping and making do, and in came a world of consumerism motivated by variety, not uniformity. The 1960s had swept in a new optimism; man was in space and would soon walk on the moon, the first heart operation had taken place and Concorde was travelling faster than the speed of sound. The modern world had arrived.

Ladybird understood that a new generation of parents would make up the greatest share of their audience. The look and feel of Ladybird books would need to appeal to this younger, more design-savvy and fashion-conscious consumer. With this in mind, Ladybird began to commission contemporary illustrators and graphic artists also working in the fields of advertising and promotional campaigns. Ladybird was in need of a fresher and more up-to-date look, and this generation of artists and illustrators would create the visual aesthetic to mirror the changes in society.

Because of this, by the 1960s and 1970s many of Ladybird's books, whilst using the same level of craftmanship in the writing and illustration, reflected a greater awareness of a changing Britain.

An example of the modern family
living room, as portrayed in
The Story of Furniture
601 Achievements, 1971.
Original artwork by Robert Ayton.

Modern Lifestyle

4c Say the Sound
641 Key Words, 1965.
Illustrations by
J. H. Wingfield

9b Jump From the Sky
641 Key Words, 1966.
Illustrations by
Martin Aitchison

Harry Wingfield and Martin Aitchison's illustrations for the Key Words Reading Scheme depicted Peter and Jane living an ordinary everyday existence, yet increasingly surrounded by the trappings of an idealized and modernist lifestyle. These ranged from the lemon-yellow Mini in *4c Say the Sound* and the futuristic slide projector in *9b Jump from the Sky* to the space ship and astronauts of *11b The Carnival*.

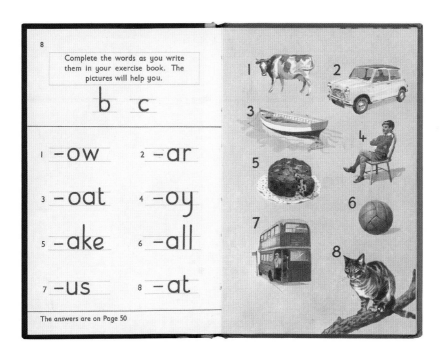

4c *Say the Sound*
641 Key Words, 1965.
Illustrations by
J. H. Wingfield

9b *Jump From the Sky*
641 Key Words, 1966.
Illustrations by
Martin Aitchison.

11b The Carnival
641 Key Words, 1967.
Illustrations by
Martin Aitchison.

8

Simon's friend used blue chalk for the background of his drawing. "We can paint the wires blue so that they will not be seen," he said. "It is a good idea to use a blue background," said John, "because the sky is blue."

"We must remember that there are two processions," said another of the boys. "One is in the early afternoon, and the other much later when it is dark. We should have lights to show up the space ship and the astronauts. There should also be flashing lights on the space ship."

"Let's make a list of all the things we need," said Simon. He got a piece of paper and a pencil and started to write. The others helped him with the list. Then he pinned it on the wall by the plan.

The next thing to do was to get the tools, wood, paint and other things needed for the work they were going to do. This took the rest of the day.

They all found that most people were glad to give them what they could. Everyone knew about the carnival and the procession. The money it would make was to help poor children and old people in need.

Ladybird by Design

Architecture and Fashion

Changing London fashions
of the 1960s.

Many of Ladybird's illustrators – primarily men in the middle years of their lives – were to visually reflect within their illustrations the changing times they were experiencing themselves. The pace of change would probably have been felt quite acutely by a generation of commercial artists who had lived through the Second World War and were now witnessing the relative prosperity of the late 1950s and the 1960s.

The birth of rock and roll, the invention of the teenager and the introduction of emerging technologies, such as the television and the telephone, indicated that a bright and shiny future was fast approaching. With the clearing of Victorian slum housing and bomb-sites to make way for modernist high-rise flats and social housing developments, Britain was entering a new era, and Ladybird, sometimes overtly but more often quite subtly, was instrumental in showing this brave new world.

Fashion too was changing radically and Ladybird's illustrators captured the new sense of freedom that the 'swinging sixties' ushered in. The prim and proper 1950s housewife

*The Story of
Houses and Homes
601 Achievements, 1963.
Illustrations by
Robert Ayton.*

gave way to an altogether groovier 1960s fashion-conscious wife and mother – colours were sharper, and the look more dramatic. Ladybird was reflecting the zeitgeist.

Ladybird's depiction of the changing face of fashion, architecture, technology and leisure time portrayed the era in a positive light. Little mention was made of any social problems, such as the impact of the 1970s recession or the bleak oppression of the Cold War. Ladybird's relentless optimism remained steadfast.

In a Big Store
606B People at Work,
1973. Original artwork
by John Berry.

12

The Story of Newspapers
601 Achievements, 1969.
Illustrations by
R. Emberton.

The Story of Clothes and Costume
601 Achievements, 1964.
Illustrations by Robert Ayton.

An Illustrated Life

It would be impossible to identify any one series that fully encapsulates the Ladybird aesthetic or ethos. There were so many titles over such a broad range of themes, ideas and interests, and in such a variety of visual approaches that attempting to distil the books into a single title or series would be fruitless.

Certainly, there were key visual elements that gave consistency to the list. Illustrations were always executed with exacting precision and a real attention to detail. The fifty-six-page format also provided a generalized visual aesthetic, with text on the verso (left-hand) page and full-colour illustrations on the recto (right-hand) page a consistent feature throughout many of Ladybird's books.

The rigid framework of the format, however, allowed for huge flexibility across artwork styles. From Tunnicliffe's detailed landscape paintings of the British countryside in *The Farm* and the infographics, tables and charts by Robert Ayton for *Your Body* to Eric Winter's accurate representation of creative projects in *Learning to Sew* and G. Robinson's rather random and surreal objects depicted in *The Ladybird Book of Things to Make*, Ladybird's gifted artists brought each subject to life with a rounded approach to realism. The images were accurate, of course, but they were always endearing and exuded warmth.

Ladybird was a brand to be trusted. Whilst modern and forward-looking, Ladybird also understood the link that its audience had with its past; that children's books were to be enjoyed by parent and child alike, and that they would bond through the shared experience. Ladybird knew that to fully engage and captivate a child the calibre and quality of the artworks would have to be second to none. If the books' aesthetic appealed to children, then their parents would readily purchase them – the wholesome illustrations, and the illustrated covers in particular, acted as a visual encouragement to get parents reading with their offspring.

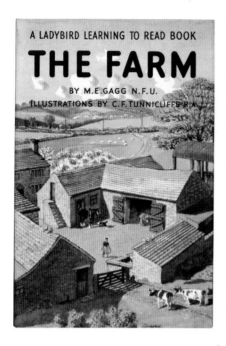

The Farm
563 Learning to Read, 1958. Illustrations by C. F. Tunnicliffe.

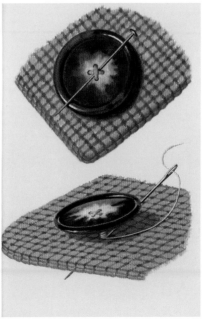

Learning to Sew
633 Hobbies and Interests, 1972. Illustrations by Eric Winter.

The Ladybird Book of
Things to Make
633 Hobbies and Interests, 1963.
Original artwork by G. Robinson.

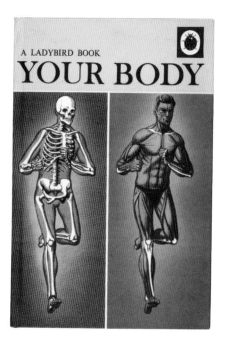

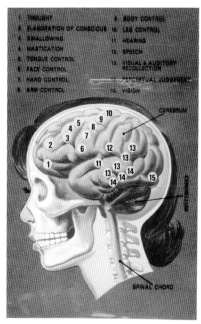

Your Body
536 Nature, 1967.
Illustrations by Robert Ayton

The Muscles

Every joint in your body is controlled by *muscles*, which are bundles of fibres forming the flesh. Muscles are usually in the shape of long, thin cells called fibres. They are fastened to the joints by strong cords of fibrous tissue, called *tendons*.

Muscles are arranged in layers, one on top of the other, intricately and wonderfully positioned to give efficient control to every moving part of the body. Movement is brought about by contracting or relaxing the muscles. When you bend your elbow you can feel the hard lump of contracted muscle called the biceps, under the skin. The muscles give strength to the limbs, and the stronger your muscles, the stronger you are.

Every time you bend your arm or move your wrist or fingers, you use the muscles in your arm. You use muscles when you walk or run, turn your head, bend down, or make any movement. The muscles in your face enable you to change your expression; to laugh, grin, cry, blink or twitch your nose. Your strong jaw muscles are used when you eat or talk.

Some muscles operate without you knowing, as much when you are asleep as awake. These control your breathing, digestion, the working of your heart and so on.

8

Above
SHOWS WHERE THE
BICEPS ARE JOINED
TO THE BONES.

1. CLAVICLE (Collar bone)
2. HUMERUS
3. SCAPULA
4. BICEPS
5. HUMERUS
6. RADIUS
7. ULNA

Well-loved Tales

For children who grew up in Britain in the 1960s and 1970s the Well-loved Tales are likely to be some of the most recognizable of all Ladybird books. This series, 606D, was certainly very popular. Its original list comprised twenty-seven traditional fairy tales published between 1964 and 1974. There were also another five titles added up to 1980 and further reprints in subsequent years, some with different covers and illustrations.

The popularity of this series was in the distinctive retelling of traditional fairy stories and the beauty of the accompanying illustrations, in the main created by Eric Winter and Robert Lumley. Vera Southgate, an English teacher, retold the first twenty-seven stories of the series with the remaining five books authored by Vernon Mills, Lynne Bradbury, Audrey Daly and Enid C. King.

Well-loved Tales today remains one of the most collectible of the Ladybird series. The first title, *Cinderella* – the only title in the series to be issued with a dust jacket and not a coloured board cover – is particularly sought after.

Educating parents and teachers as well as young readers was important to Ladybird. The titles in series 606D were listed on the back cover of each book and given a grade between 1 and 3, which signified the level of reading difficulty for children. Classified as part of the Easy-Reading series, the message to parents on the inside cover was as much a sales pitch as it was an encouragement to read with and to their children. 'This is one of the stories that children have always loved,' states one book's text. 'The younger ones will enjoy seeing the full-colour illustrations and having the story read to them. Older children who need reading practice will be encouraged by the clear type and relatively simple text,' it continues.

The illustrations were engaging and realistic – Puss stands tall and proud in a supremely convincing manner in Eric Winter's illustrations for *Puss in Boots*, first published in 1967, whilst Robert Lumley's quirky pancake in *The Big Pancake,* published in 1972, escapes the pan and rolls down hills chased by a mother and her chain of seven hungry sons. The fairy tales, recounted by Southgate in charming prose throughout the series, are illustrated sympathetically, with the moral of the story or happy ending of each tale perfectly encapsulated in each closing image.

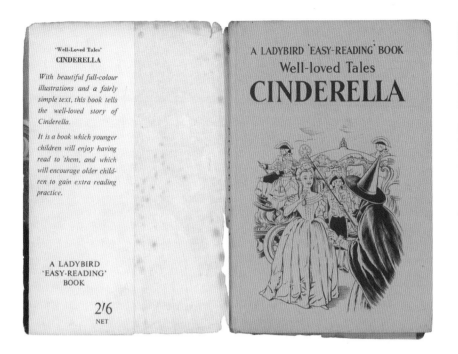

'Well-Loved Tales'
CINDERELLA

With beautiful full-colour illustrations and a fairly simple text, this book tells the well-loved story of Cinderella.

It is a book which younger children will enjoy having read to 'them, and which will encourage older children to gain extra reading practice.

A LADYBIRD
'EASY-READING'
BOOK

2/6
NET

A LADYBIRD 'EASY-READING' BOOK
Well-loved Tales
CINDERELLA

LEFT: First-edition dust jacket and printed cover board, 1964. *Cinderella* was the only title in series 606D to be originally published with a dust jacket as Ladybird stopped using them in 1965.

ABOVE: Reissued *Cinderella* with colour cover and no dust jacket.
606D Well-loved Tales, *c.*1965.
Illustrations by Eric Winter.

From Eric Winter's Rumpelstiltskin and his portrait of Dick Whittington as the Lord Mayor of London to Robert Lumley's image of Foxy Loxy and family resting comfortably after having devoured Chicken Licken and friends, the illustrations both complement and extend the story for the young reader, bringing each tale to life.

The illustrated images for Well-loved Tales were to become the de facto visual interpretation of traditional fairy tales – a balance of believable realism with a twist of the macabre and surreal. In essence, it was a perfect balance for the unbridled imagination of Ladybird's junior readers (and their parents too, of course).

Now it happened that the King arranged a great feast for his son. The feast was to last three days and on each evening there was to be a grand ball. All the beautiful young girls in the country were invited, in order that the Prince might choose himself a bride.

Cinderella's sisters were invited to the feast and they were so excited that they could talk of nothing else. Cinderella was not invited. As she was only seen in rags, working in the kitchen, everyone thought that she was her sisters' maid.

On the evening of the first ball, Cinderella had to help her sisters to put on their new dresses and arrange their hair.

8

When Cinderella arrived at the palace, she looked so beautiful that the ugly sisters did not know her. They thought she must be a princess from another country. They never thought of Cinderella, for they believed that she was sitting at home, by the cinders.

The prince thought that he had never seen such a beautiful princess. He came towards Cinderella, took her hand and danced with her. All evening he would dance with no other maiden, and he never let her out of his sight. If anyone else came to invite her to dance, the prince said, "This is my partner."

26

When Cinderella arrived at the ball, in her dress of silver and gold, she looked so magnificent that no one knew how to speak for astonishment.

The prince danced with no-one but Cinderella all evening and, if anyone invited her to dance, he said, "This is my partner." Cinderella was so happy that she forgot all about the time.

Suddenly the clock began to strike twelve. Cinderella was terrified that she would find herself in the ballroom in her old grey dress. She rushed out of the door in such haste that she lost her slipper.

The prince ran after her and saw the slipper. He picked it up, and it was small and dainty and all golden.

40

Cinderella first washed her hands and face clean and then went and bowed down before the prince, who gave her the golden shoe. She seated herself on her stool, drew her foot out of the heavy wooden shoe, and put it into the slipper, which fitted like a glove.

When Cinderella stood up and the prince looked at her face, he knew it was the beautiful maiden who had danced with him. He cried out, "This is the true bride."

At that moment, Cinderella's fairy godmother appeared and turned her once more into the beautiful princess. The old grey dress became a velvet gown.

The prince lifted Cinderella on to his horse and rode away with her.

48

II. A Design for Life

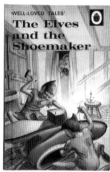

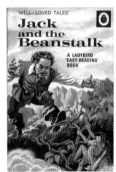

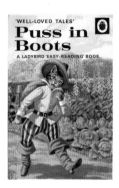

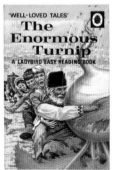

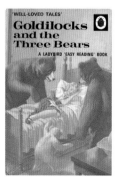

BOTH PAGES:
606D Well-loved Tales,
various covers, 1964–1974.
Illustrations by John Berry,
Capaldi, Robert Lumley
and Eric Winter.

Ladybird by Design

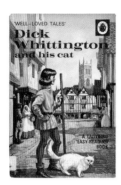

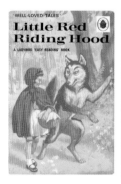

Fairy-tale Baddies

The fairy tale is often quite simply a story of good overcoming evil; the premise remains extremely popular and the enjoyment this has given generations of children has ensured its longevity. New formats and platforms may emerge, but the key elements of the fairy-tale plot remain.

   The secrets to a good fairy tale are a strong storyline – often with a positive moral outcome – as well as a heroine and/or hero that the reader can identify with or aspire to be like. The third vital ingredient is the villain. The typical baddie will display negative and destructive behavioural traits; they're often manipulative or jealous and obsessed with wreaking revenge on the hero or heroine of the story. Their attire also signifies evil: often dressed in black with a cloak or hood to hide their face, there is no mistaking a fairy-tale villain. These baddies are many children's first introduction to the struggle between good and bad behaviour. Whilst simplistic characterizations, fairy-tale characters allow elements of evil to be shown within a safe environment. They enable young readers to experience some degree of fear from a safe distance whilst showing them the benefits of ultimately choosing the right moral path.

Jack and the Beanstalk
606D Well-loved Tales,
1965. Illustrations
by Eric Winter.

Little Red Riding Hood
606D Well-loved Tales,
1972. Illustrations
by Eric Winter.

Ladybird by Design

Rumpelstiltskin
606D Well-loved Tales,
1968. Illustrations by Eric Winter.

Sleeping Beauty
606D Well-loved Tales,
1965. Illustrations by Eric Winter.

The Three Little Pigs
606D Well-loved Tales,
1965. Illustrations by
Robert Lumley.

The Gingerbread Boy
606D Well-loved Tales,
1966. Illustrations by
Robert Lumley.

Eric Winter

Rumpelstiltskin
606D Well-loved Tales,
1968. Illustrations
by Eric Winter.

Eric Winter is perhaps best known for illustrating some of the most popular Ladybird titles, including *Cinderella, Jack and the Beanstalk, Rapunzel* and *The Princess and the Pea* from the Well-loved Tales series (606D).

Born in 1905 in Edmonton in Essex and educated at Latymer School, Winter went on to study at Hornsey School of Art. There he specialized in commercial and fine art, painting in oils and water-colours, and drawing in charcoal.

Working as a commercial artist after graduation, Winter was commissioned in the 1950s by the Abbey National Building Society, and created the famous graphic image of two people sheltering under the roof of a house.

Winter also worked as a commercial artist for various magazines, including *Woman's Own, Woman* and *The Girl* and was also commissioned to create illustrations for the *Eagle* comic. Winter was first signed up by Ladybird in 1970, and he created many illustrations for classic fairy tales. Some of Winter's watercolours have been exhibited at the Royal Academy of Arts. He died in 1981.

Rapunzel
606D Well-loved Tales, 1968.
Illustrations by Eric Winter.

The Princess and the Pea
606D Well-loved Tales, 1967.
Illustrations by Eric Winter.

Robert Lumley

Well-loved Tales illustrator Robert Lumley was born in Southwark, London in 1920. After studying at Hammersmith Art College, where John Berry was one of his contemporaries, Lumley served in the Second World War, seeing active service in North Africa and Italy. After the war, Lumley worked as an apprentice under David Hand, the art director of Disney's *Bambi*.

Lumley's ten-year relationship with Ladybird began in 1964 with a commission to create the illustrations for *The Elves and the Shoemaker*. Lumley's most-loved illustrations are possibly the set he created for *The Three Little Pigs*. He put his son to work researching caricatures of pigs and wolves in a copy of *The Art of Walt Disney*, and the influences of Disney's animations are clear in Lumley's finished artwork.

For subsequent commissions, Lumley moved away from caricatures and looked to draw animals and people more realistically. He would study and draw animals and often photographed and used locals from his village as models for his work on Well-loved Tales. The baker in *The Little Red Hen and the Grains of Wheat* was drawn from the village baker posing in front of his shop, the butcher in *The Old Woman and her Pig* was his local butcher, and the seven hungry boys in *The Big Pancake* were the sons of the local headmaster, the vicar, a farm worker and the village policeman.

Sadly, Lumley's career as a book illustrator was cut short: having stopped illustrating for Ladybird in 1973 he was tragically killed in a road-traffic accident in 1976.

The Three Little Pigs 606D Well-loved Tales, 1965. Illustrations by Robert Lumley.

The Little Red Hen and the Grains of Wheat
606D Well-loved Tales, 1966. Illustrations by Robert Lumley.

The Old Woman and her Pig
606D Well-loved Tales, 1973. Illustrations by Robert Lumley.

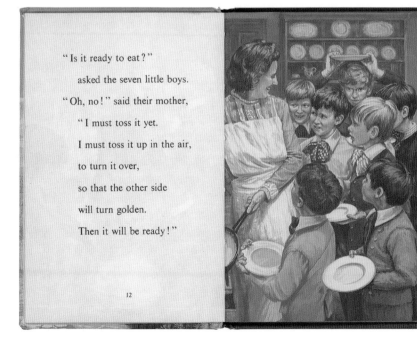

"Is it ready to eat?"

asked the seven little boys.

"Oh, no!" said their mother,

"I must toss it yet.

I must toss it up in the air,

to turn it over,

so that the other side

will turn golden.

Then it will be ready!"

12

The Big Pancake
606D Well-loved Tales, 1972. Illustrations by Robert Lumley.

Key Words Reading Scheme

William Murray, head teacher and creator of the bestselling Key Words Reading Scheme.

Both the bestselling and longest-running series in Ladybird history is the Key Words Reading Scheme, commonly known as the Peter and Jane books. Almost 100 million copies had been sold in Britain and across the world at the time of Ladybird's 100th anniversary in 2015, with export sales particularly high in Pakistan, India and Singapore.

Douglas Keen, editorial director until 1973, was instrumental in developing the series for Ladybird following a lecture he attended in 1963 given by William Murray, the head teacher of a Cheltenham-based school and an international lecturer in child development and reading. Murray presented a paper, 'Key Words to Literacy', which explained a method for teaching children to read based on the systematic introduction of commonly occurring words. Keen saw in this theory the potential for a series of books.

Murray conducted the research with Joe McNally, an educational psychologist, and established that only twelve words make up twenty-five per cent of spoken English: *a*, *and*, *he*, *I*, *in*, *is*, *it*, *of*, *that*, *the*, *to*, and *was*. They then concluded that 100 words accounted for fifty per cent of the spoken English language, and that an additional 300 words made up seventy-five per cent of spoken English. Children therefore would learn to read more quickly and easily if they learnt these words first.

Equipped with Murray and McNally's theory, Douglas Keen persuaded Murray to author a series of books for Ladybird. Murray was enthusiastic about the user-friendly Ladybird format with its full-colour illustrations as a way of implementing his teaching method, especially when Keen presented him with sample pages of the books created by illustrator Harry Wingfield. Just as when Keen had shown the prototype of *A Book of Birds & Eggs* to the Ladybird board, here was another design dummy that helped to instigate a new series.

The full set of Key Words Reading Scheme books totalled thirty-six titles in three series, numbered 1a to 12c: the 'a' books introduced words using a simple storybook format; the 'b' books used different contexts to repeat the words; and the 'c' books identified and introduced writing skills and phonetics.

The task of illustrating the majority of the thirty-six titles fell to Harry Wingfield and Martin Aitchison, with a minority of titles illustrated by John Berry and Robert Ayton. The overall cost of commissioning the artwork in

Purposeful writing generally awakens interest and often stimulates enthusiasm.

Individual Record and Reading Test Card

The Ladybird Key Words Reading Scheme Individual Record Card and Reading Test provides an easy-to-keep record of books read, with space for notes by the teacher. The Reading Test, which is on the reverse side of the Card and covers the first six stages of the Scheme, has identical letter shapes and print sizes to those found in the books.

Teaching Reading was a comprehensive parent and teacher guide developed by Murray to accompany the Key Words Reading Scheme. The image to the left is an excerpt from the book showing the most common key words in written and spoken English, as used in the series. Reading the books in order from 1a to 12c and practising all of these words gives children the sufficient independent reading skills to read a daily newspaper.

Teaching Reading
642 Key Words Picture Dictionaries, 1969.

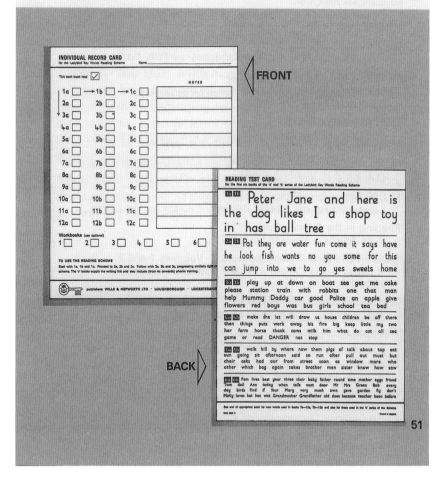

FRONT

BACK

51

7a Happy Holiday
641 Key Words, 1964.
Illustrations by
J. H. Wingfield.

2c I Like to Write
641 Key Words, 1965.
Illustrations by
Martin Aitchison.

3c Let Me Write
641 Key Words, 1965.
Illustrations by
Martin Aitchison.

5b Out in the Sun
641 Key Words, 1965.
Illustrations by
Frank Hampson.

1964 was reported to have been £25,000 – more than £450,000 in today's money. Artists were usually contracted on a flat-fee buy-out basis, but the costs involved represented a significant financial commitment by the Ladybird board. It also meant that some of Ladybird's regular, trusted artists were tied up on the project so that new illustrators had to be sourced from agencies and other areas to work on other titles. Douglas Keen's reputation and career was potentially at risk if the project were to fail.

Work on the titles began in 1964 and was completed by 1968. New machines had to be purchased to keep up with the demand of printing so many titles, and earlier books were stored in stockrooms until the full series was available to sell. The Ladybird Key Words Reading Scheme was a huge success, with the series sold in bookshops, toy shops and newsagents, and to schools and libraries. The company claimed that millions of children learned to read using the books, with the scheme playing a vital role in the education of British children during the 1960s and 1970s.

Murray went on to write two further successful reading schemes for Ladybird, Read with Me and Sunstart, both of which are still in print. In all, Murray wrote over seventy books for the publishers.

Despite the popularity of the Key Words Reading Scheme, the illustrations across the entire series of thirty-six books were updated in the 1970s, partly to reflect changes in fashion – Peter and Jane needed more modern styling – but also partly in response to criticism of some of the stereotypes portrayed in their world. In the later versions, we see Daddy doing the washing up, a greater ethnic mix of characters and a less overtly gendered approach to Peter and Jane's games. This artwork is still used in the books today.

1c Read and Write (reillustration)
641 Key Words, 1975.
Illustrations by J. H. Wingfield.

2c I Like to Write (reillustration)
641 Key Words, 1977.
Illustrations by Martin Aitchison.

3c Let Me Write (reillustration)
641 Key Words, 1972.
Illustrations by Martin Aitchison.

3c Let Me Write (reillustration)
641 Key Words, 1972.
Illustrations by Martin Aitchison.

1c Read and Write
641 Key Words, 1965.
Illustrations by J. H. Wingfield.

14

The children are in the house in the tree. The dog is with the children.

"Let us have tea here," says Jane. "That will be fun," she says.

"Yes," says Peter, "you make the tea. I will draw. I will draw some flowers."

"Yes, I will be like Mummy and get the tea," says Jane. "I like to get the tea."

no new words

4a Things We Do
641 Key Words, 1964.
Illustrations by J. H. Wingfield.

12

Peter and Jane
like the dog.
I like the dog.

the dog

1b Look At This
641 Key Words, 1964.
Illustrations by J. H. Wingfield.

The Real Peter and Jane

1c Read and Write
641 Key Words, 1965.
Illustrations by J. H. Wingfield.

Peter and Jane are probably the most familiar of all characters to have existed within the pages of Ladybird books. The stars of the Key Words Reading Scheme, Peter and Jane live with their parents and their pet dog, Pat, in middle-class suburbia. They have an idyllic lifestyle, where summer holidays are sunny and never-ending, and where adventures in the woods or at the beach are informative and interesting.

Peter's role model is his father, who works hard at the office – for Daddy isn't engaged in the type of manual labour depicted in the People at Work titles – and is home at six o'clock to read the daily newspaper, whilst Jane's role model, her mother, cleans, cooks and bakes.

Across the Key Words Reading Scheme a total of four illustrators were commissioned to breathe life into Peter and Jane's adventures. Harry Wingfield and Martin Aitchison illustrated the majority of the 1960s titles, with the remaining books illustrated by John Berry and Robert Ayton – who followed Wingfield's original style to ensure uniformity between different titles.

Despite different working methods, what connected each illustrator in terms of approach was their dedication to researching their subjects. Drawing from life or photographic reference was vital – particularly for body proportions, for example.

However, whilst it is nice to imagine that Peter and Jane were real children, they were actually the product of the four illustrators' imaginations and Douglas Keen – his brief was that they should be the children next door, utterly normal yet resolutely well-behaved and positive individuals.

Of the four illustrators working on the series only Harry Wingfield divulged details of his models. They were local children Jill Ashurst and Christopher Edwards, from the same town as Wingfield, Sutton Coldfield. During their summer holidays, Wingfield built a photographic archive of the two children doing everyday tasks – washing dishes, gardening, and playing football and tennis, to use as reference for illustrations later in the year. When Wingfield required reference but Jill and Christopher were unavailable, he would turn to other children he knew.

8

Jane wants to play.

I want to play, please,
Jane says.

Peter, I want to jump,
please.

Jane jumps up and down.

Up and down I go,
Jane says.

Up and down, up and
down.

Look at me, Peter.

please   down

3b *Boys and Girls*
641 Key Words, 1964.
Illustrations by Robert Ayton.

34

"Come to the house and see my daddy draw," says the other girl to Jane.

They go to the house and go up to see her daddy at work. He sits on a chair as he works. A cat is on the other chair.

As the girl's daddy draws he talks to them.

"Have you had some fun?" he asks.

They talk to him about the walk they had, and the things they saw.

"Now Jane and I are going for a walk with the boys," says the girl to her daddy.

They go down with the boys. The boys have a bag to take with them.

There are apples in the bag.

bag

5b *Out in the Sun*
641 Key Words, 1965.
Illustrations by Frank Hampson.

Martin Aitchison

Martin Aitchison was one of Ladybird's most prolific illustrators. His work appeared in almost 100 titles, including Key Words (series 641), where he joined Harry Wingfield, John Berry and Robert Ayton in bringing Peter and Jane to life, Well-loved Tales (series 606D), Puddle Lane (series 855) and Great Artists (series 701). He became a freelance illustrator for Ladybird in 1963, the same year that *Eagle*, a comic he had worked on alongside other Ladybird illustrators Frank Hampson and Frank Humphris, folded.

Born in 1919 in Birmingham and educated at Ellesmere College in Shropshire, Aitchison's deafness, later profound, was a hindrance to his academic education and he left school at fifteen to develop his artistic talents at Birmingham School of Art and later at the Slade School of Art.

Unable to enlist for military service during the Second World War, Aitchison instead enrolled as a technical illustrator for Vickers Aircraft. He produced service manuals and was also involved in creating technical illustrations for Barnes Wallis's top-secret project, the 'Bouncing Bomb', used in the famous Dam Busters raid.

Following the war, Aitchison became a freelance commercial artist working for advertising agencies and other clients, including the women's magazine *Vogue*. In 1952, he joined *Eagle* for an eleven-year period, illustrating *Luck of the Legion* as well as other serialized comic strips.

His entry into working with Ladybird in 1963, however, wasn't a smooth one: his very first test illustration was rejected. Eager to join the ranks at Ladybird, Aitchison returned to his studio and worked hard to create an illustration style that suited the Ladybird aesthetic. When he stopped illustrating for Ladybird in 1987 after twenty-four years, Aitchison continued to work for Oxford University Press and other clients until his retirement.

8c Fun With Sounds
641 Key Words, 1966.
Illustrations by Martin Aitchison.

Great Artists Book 1
701 Great Artists, 1970.
Illustrations by Martin Aitchison.

Out into the snow marched Dennis.
It was cold for dragon toes.
Then he breathed and puffed quite gently,
Till a flame came from his nose.

Dennis the Dragon
401 Animal Stories, 1980.
Illustrations by Martin Aitchison.

Learning to Read

Making learning and education enjoyable and accessible was at the centre of the Ladybird rationale; and reading, above all else, was considered to be the gateway to all future knowledge. Prior to the introduction of the Key Words Reading Scheme in 1964, Ladybird had ventured into helping children to read with the Learning to Read books (series 563), published between 1956 and 1962. Focused on appealing to parents as pre-school educators, the series aimed to capitalize on Wills & Hepworth's reputation as publishers of high-quality texts.

Comprising nine titles, the Learning to Read series offered beginner readers picture books with simple corresponding texts, usually no more than a few words or a single sentence. The books, each of them 'specially designed by an expert', utilized a large typeface and widely spaced letters, which were formulated to ensure ease of reading. Like the Key Words Reading Scheme, which emphasized the expertise of educationists William Murray and Joe McNally, the expert engaged in writing the Learning to Read books, Margaret Elise Gagg, was well-known in the educational world.

The books were designed sympathetically for the intended audience. 'The words have been carefully chosen,' explains the introduction to *Shopping with Mother*, the third book in the series, 'and the delightful pictures skilfully matched with the text'. The carefully chosen words were also frequently repeated to enable young readers to recognize the structure of words and their relationship with the visual imagery – 'everything is designed to help beginners to work out for themselves the simple but enjoyable reading matter,' explains the text in *The Farm*.

The Farm, published in 1958, was the first of five books illustrated by Charles Tunnicliffe before he moved on to create the artwork for the following titles in Ladybird's iconic Nature series (536): *What to Look for in Winter* in 1959, *What to Look for in Summer* and *What to Look for in Autumn* in 1960 and *What to Look for in Spring* in 1961.

Whilst the subject matter throughout the series was varied, there was real consistency in the sense of fun and engagement each book was to have with its readers. The Learning to Read books were popular for their humble storylines and captivating images, with text that aimed to introduce the pleasure of reading to a young audience not yet confident enough to read alone.

20

Puppies and Kittens
563 Learning to Read,
1956. Original artwork
by Harry Woolley.

Puppies and Kittens
563 Learning to Read, 1956.
Illustrations by
Harry Woolley.

This puppy
can see a robin.

These kittens
want to write.

Numbers
563 Learning to Read,
1959. Illustrations
by G. Robinson.

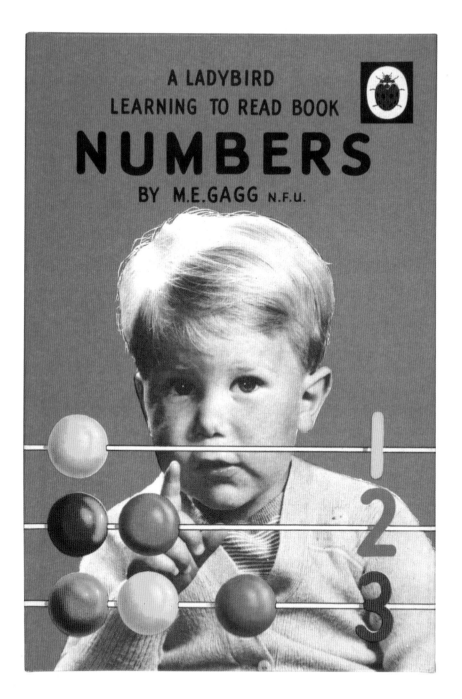

A LADYBIRD
LEARNING TO READ BOOK

NUMBERS

BY M.E.GAGG N.F.U.

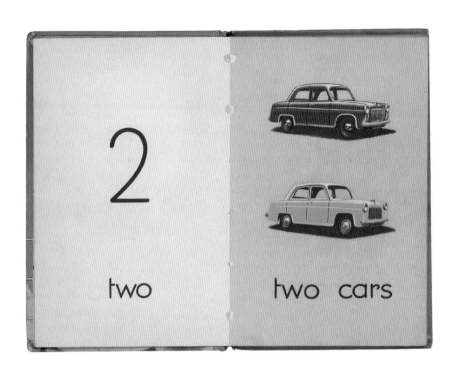

2

two

two cars

How many
milk bottles ?

The Zoo
563 Learning to Read, 1960.
Illustrations by Barry Driscoll.

The penguins
like fish too.

46

The Party
563 Learning to Read, 1960.
Illustrations by J. H. Wingfield.

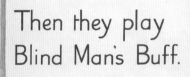

Then they play
Blind Man's Buff.

Learning with Mother

Ladybird's traditional take on family values during the 1960s and 1970s may now, half a century later, seem rather outdated, but the nuclear family was a key concept during Ladybird's most successful period. In the Ladybird world the family consisted of a mother and father living in suburban bliss with their two children and pet dog. Father went out to work and Mother stayed at home as homemaker and housewife. Ladybird understood that the bond between pre-school child and stay-at-home mother, where the mother took a leading role in educating her offspring, was one that could provide a fruitful source of revenue.

Learning with Mother (series 702) comprised sixteen titles published between 1970 and 1979. Just as the Key Words series was a reading scheme for everyday British children, so Learning with Mother – which was first published some seven years later – was the series that ingrained into the British psyche that under-fives required greater mental stimulation than previously thought. 'Almost half of your child's intelligence will be decided by four and a half!' read the startling text on the opening pages of the first Learning with Mother books.

The first five books in the series were to be a collaboration between established Ladybird illustrator Harry Wingfield and his wife Ethel, a primary school teacher, who provided the text. The texts for each of these books offered positive and informative advice for mothers, helping them to acknowledge and support the rapid month-by-month development of their small child's learning.

Harry Wingfield's beautifully illustrated depictions of young mothers with their under-fives are heart-warming and engaging; the children are active and happy and their mothers fashionable and carefree. Of course, the children are clean and well-nourished and their mothers independent and time-rich, cheerful as they wash the dishes or hang out the clothes to dry, apparently enjoying the everyday.

The relationship between mother and child appears to be nothing short of idyllic; Ladybird's text and images seemingly the key ingredients in ensuring a happy and fruitful learning experience through carefully constructed play. With these books, Ladybird was to encourage a growing theory that intellectual improvement through play was an intrinsic part of developing a child's intelligence prior to and during the early stages of school.

Learning with Mother Book 1
702 Learning with Mother, 1970.
Illustrations by J. H. Wingfield.

Learning with Mother Book 1
702 Learning with Mother,
1970. Illustrations by
J. H. Wingfield.

The Best Start in Life

The first five Learning with Mother books were designed to be read by adults interested in ensuring that their children had the best start in life. A child's development was plotted out month by month – in Book 1, for example, a mother could learn about her child's development from the age of three months to two years, with key tips and advice for each and every stage. Activities varied from title to title depending on the child's age; whether singing, drawing, or learning to tell the time, the books concentrated on building a child's confidence and knowledge through play and experimentation.

Learning with Mother Book 2
702 Learning with Mother,
1970. Illustrations by
J. H. Wingfield.

Learning with Mother Book 3
702 Learning with Mother,
1970. Illustrations by
J. H. Wingfield.

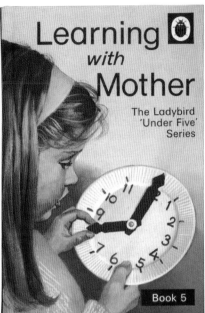

Learning with Mother Book 4
702 Learning with Mother,
1971. Illustrations by
J. H. Wingfield.

Learning with Mother Book 5
702 Learning with Mother,
1972. Illustrations by
J. H. Wingfield.

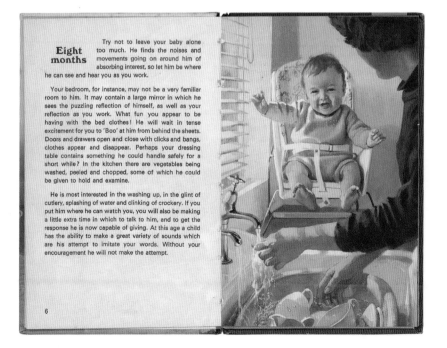

Learning with Mother Book 1
702 Learning with Mother,
1970. Illustrations by
J. H. Wingfield.

**Eight
months**

Try not to leave your baby alone too much. He finds the noises and movements going on around him of absorbing interest, so let him be where he can see and hear you as you work.

Your bedroom, for instance, may not be a very familiar room to him. It may contain a large mirror in which he sees the puzzling reflection of himself, as well as your reflection as you work. What fun you appear to be having with the bed clothes! He will wait in tense excitement for you to 'Boo' at him from behind the sheets. Doors and drawers open and close with clicks and bangs, clothes appear and disappear. Perhaps your dressing table contains something he could handle safely for a short while? In the kitchen there are vegetables being washed, peeled and chopped, some of which he could be given to hold and examine.

He is most interested in the washing up, in the glint of cutlery, splashing of water and clinking of crockery. If you put him where he can watch you, you will also be making a little extra time in which to talk to him, and to get the response he is now capable of giving. At this age a child has the ability to make a great variety of sounds which are his attempt to imitate your words. Without your encouragement he will not make the attempt.

6

Learning with Mother Book 1
702 Learning with Mother, 1970.
Illustrations by J. H. Wingfield.

Harry Wingfield

The artist behind the first five Learning with Mother titles also brought to life the much-loved brother and sister duo of the Key Words Reading Scheme, Peter and Jane.

Born in Denby, near Derby, in December 1910, John Henry Wingfield came to prominence as a portrait artist painting pictures of his colleagues and family whilst working as a driver in the RAF during the Second World War. He had previously worked for an advertising agency (where he first met Douglas Keen), and attended evening classes in drawing to perfect his craft, before turning to a career as a freelance graphic artist.

Wingfield's wholesome and detailed depictions of Peter and Jane resonated with the public. He enjoyed drawing from life, often using local children playing on the new West Midlands council estates close to where he lived as studies for his final watercolour artworks.

Wingfield created illustrations for other Ladybird titles, such as Junior Science (series 621), as well as *Goldilocks and the Three Bears* and *Little Red Riding Hood* for Well-loved Tales (series 606D). For the latter, he created believable characters and scenes for

9a Games We Like
641 Key Words, 1964.
Illustrations by J. H. Wingfield.

traditional tales. However, it wasn't the escapism of this work that he would be best remembered for, but rather his work for the Key Words Reading Scheme, which has sold 100 million copies to date. Wingfield died in 2002 at the age of ninety-one.

LEARNING WITH TRADITIONAL RHYMES

Memory Rhymes

Learning with Rhymes

The later books in the Learning with Mother series were published in the 1970s and were for mothers to read to and with their children. *Memory Rhymes*, *Action Rhymes*, *Finger Rhymes*, *Number Rhymes*, *Talking Rhymes* and *Dancing Rhymes* all mixed illustrations with photographic images. The photos demonstrated to adults the importance of play and interaction with their child, and the illustrations encouraged children to engage fully with the book whilst learning and reciting the rhymes.

Finger Rhymes
702 Learning with Mother, 1976. Illustrations by Brian Price Thomas. Photography by John Moyes.

Row, row, row your boat

Row, row, row your boat,
Gently down the stream.
Merrily, merrily, merrily, merrily,
Life is but a dream.

Action Rhymes
702 Learning with Mother, 1976. Illustrations by Kathy Layfield and Brian Price Thomas. Photography by John Moyes.

Animal Stories

Ladybird's very first venture into the small hardback format during the early years of the Second World War was with a set of tales depicting animals as humanized characters. Published in 1940, *Bunnikin's Picnic Party* was the first title in Animal Stories Told in Verse (series 401). Written and illustrated by Anguisine Jeanne MacGregor, with verses by W. Perring, the animal tales featured charming characters involved in amusing activities. The illustrations were designed to captivate Ladybird's young audience as the reader recited the rhyming verses.

Anguisine MacGregor's illustrations have a timeless appeal – the illustrations of Piggly, a rather naughty young piglet playing truant from school, are engaging and endearing portraits. The depictions of Downy Duckling, a less-than-bright young duckling who ends up slipping on a snowy river bank and disappearing under icy water, also capture the essence of illustration in the late 1930s and early 1940s, yet remain as delightful today as when they were first published.

It is little wonder that these first Ladybird books in the new hardback format are amongst the most collectible many decades later. They capture an innocence in children's book publishing and the tone of the stories is often highly moralistic, blatantly warning of the dangers of naughtiness: playing truant, stepping on to frozen ponds, or taking boats out to sea unaccompanied. Here were books that featured young animals behaving badly and suffering the consequences of their actions – but they were always home for supper and reunited with their families for a happy ending.

The following year saw the launch of another series, Fairy Tales and Rhymes (series 413). Published in 1941, *A First Ladybird Book of Nursery Rhymes* included favourites such as 'Hickory Dickory Dock' and 'Hey Diddle Diddle', with two fairy tales appearing in *Red Riding Hood also Goldilocks and the Three Bears*.

Animals were to take the leading role again with the later Animal Stories books (series 497), first published in 1949. The series would engage young readers with a variety of animals, all with human mannerisms – mice were inquisitive, kittens mischievous, ponies discontented, ducks greedy, puppies disobedient and roosters lazy. These captivating and charming stories would continue to be published right up to the 1980s, with *Mervyn Mouse* published in 1980 and *Dennis the Dragon Finds a New Job* in 1983.

Downy Duckling
401 Animal Stories Told in Verse,
1946. Original artwork by
A. J. MacGregor.

An early edition of *Smoke and Fluff*
401 Animal Stories Told in Verse,
1941. Illustrations by
A. J. MacGregor.

Later editions of *Smoke and Fluff*
had a full-bleed printed
cover board.

SMOKE AND
FLUFF

Ladybird by Design

Smoke and Fluff
401 Animal Stories Told in Verse,
1941. Illustrations by
A. J. MacGregor.

Here they spied a handy cupboard:
    Smoke said, " Quick, Fluff! In you go!"
Quick as lightning, in they darted,
    Fluff above and Smoke below!

14

Smoke and Fluff had softly vanished!
    Mummy tugged again and frowned.
Tug! And over went the table,
    With the tea-things to the ground.

10

The Inquisitive Harvest Mouse
497 Animal Stories, 1949.
Illustrations by
P. B. Hickling.

Cocky the Lazy Rooster
497 Animal Stories, 1953.
Illustrations by
P. B. Hickling.

Mick the Disobedient Puppy
497 Animal Stories, 1952.
Illustrations by
P. B. Hickling.

Beaky the Greedy Duck
497 Animal Stories, 1951.
Illustrations by
P. B. Hickling.

Ladybird by Design

Cocky was always very busy. He looked after the hens and settled their quarrels.

"Tell me," he would say, "what is the trouble?" and very soon he would have them all friendly again.

He chased away the mice who tried to steal a few nibbles of grain, and stood on guard when the farm cats came near the chickens. Cocky was always anxious about the chickens. They were slow to run to their mothers when they were called, and might easily have been trodden on by the cows as they came in to be milked, or by the horses as they galloped out to the field.

Cocky the Lazy Rooster
497 Animal Stories,
1953. Illustrations
by P. B. Hickling.

Now Beaky was greedy, and every day, while the hens were being fed, she took care to climb out of the pond on to the bank, and so be ready to get the largest share of anything the farmer's wife brought. The other ducks knew only too well that she did this, but somehow they could never remember to be there at the same time, and Beaky took good care not to remind them.

One fine sunny morning, the white-all-over duck floated on the clear water, watching all that happened in the farmyard.

12

Beaky the Greedy Duck
497 Animal Stories,
1951. Illustrations
by P. B. Hickling.

Tootles the Taxi
413 Fairy Tales and Rhymes,
1956. Illustrations by
John Kenney.

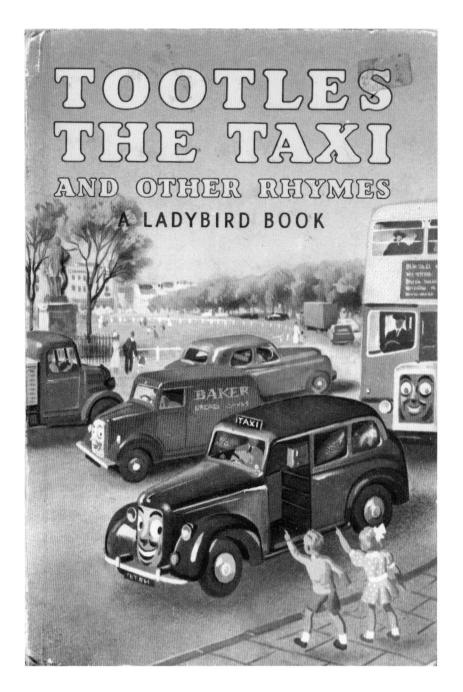

Tootles the Taxi

Humanized vehicles also came to the fore in series 413 with the introduction of the popular *Tootles the Taxi* in 1956. With verses by Joyce B. Clegg and illustrations by John Kenney, the book perhaps owes a debt in terms of visual approach to the Thomas the Tank Engine books illustrated by C. Reginald Dalby.

Interestingly, Kenney would go on to replace Dalby as the illustrator of the Thomas the Tank Engine books when Dalby parted company with the author Reverend Wilbert Awdry in 1956.

Tootles the Taxi
413 Fairy Tales and Rhymes, 1956. Original artwork by John Kenney.

Tootles the Taxi
413 Fairy Tales and Rhymes, 1956. Original sketch by John Kenney.

Tootles the Taxi
413 Fairy Tales and Rhymes,
1956. Illustrations
by John Kenney.

I'm Cuthbert the coal cart
    And I take the road,
Carrying with me
    A very big load.
After the coalman
    Has emptied the sacks,
I turn round again
    And we journey back.

38

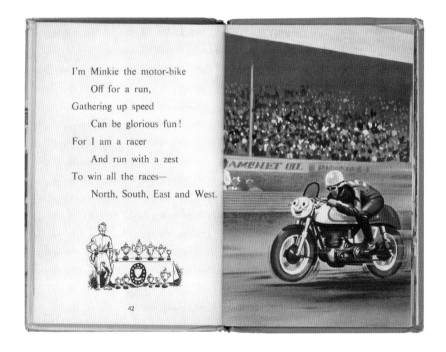

I'm Minkie the motor-bike
    Off for a run,
Gathering up speed
    Can be glorious fun!
For I am a racer
    And run with a zest
To win all the races—
    North, South, East and West.

42

The illustrations for *Tootles the Taxi* were captivating, and this style of artwork could easily have been an interesting route for Ladybird to take, but the company, and Keen in particular, opted for a more realistic art look in later series.

In 1984 a brand-new edition of *Tootles the Taxi and other rhymes* was published, with updated characters – no more Cuthbert the coal cart – and new illustrations by James Hodgson. Whilst charming in their own right, the revised rhymes and accompanying illustrations were a far cry from the characterful originals.

Tootles the Taxi,
413 Fairy Tales and Rhymes,
1984. Illustrations by
James Hodgson.

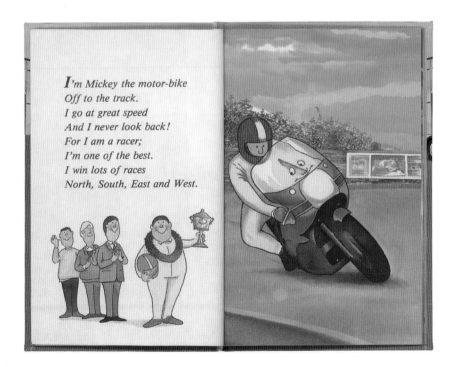

I'm Mickey the motor-bike
Off to the track.
I go at great speed
And I never look back!
For I am a racer;
I'm one of the best.
I win lots of races
North, South, East and West.

What to Look for in Autumn
536 Nature, 1960.
Illustrations by
C. F. Tunnicliffe.

Nature and Natural History

In the 1950s, Ladybird made the decision to tackle non-fiction, which would prove a successful and winning formula for the company. Douglas Keen had convinced the Ladybird directors that there was a strong demand for factual books for children, and many of the subject areas they covered were driven by his belief in the transformative power of education.

Nature and the natural world were key themes for Ladybird, reflecting as they did Douglas Keen's own interests, and were explored comprehensively through a number of books and series. These included Nature (series 536), Natural History (series 651), Animals of the World (series 691), and Conservation (series 727), and were published across four decades from the 1950s to the 1980s.

For many children and their parents, Ladybird was synonymous with nature books, and the illustrations of birds, wildlife, plants and flora were central to the success of the different series. For the young reader, learning about the natural world through Ladybird books could be fun, inspiring and so much more interesting than the rather dull and poorly illustrated books most children had access to at school or in libraries.

The accurately executed illustrations combined with well-researched text ensured that Ladybird's books on nature were taken to farmyards, fields, woods and the coastline of Great Britain. Their small size meant that they could be stashed in duffle bags, saddlebags or pockets, to be lovingly used by adventurers on holidays or day trips as spotter's guides for identifying birds, nests, wild flowers, and insects.

The design of many of the Nature books (series 536) was well considered; end-papers often presented additional facts and visual information, creating a mini-encyclopaedia of visual knowledge and an even greater sense of value for money. Silhouettes of birds in flight, line drawings of trees, diagrams of wings, feet, feathers and beaks, charts depicting the life cycle of the butterfly, the formation of clouds, animal skeletons and a structural diagram of a beehive were all additional visual materials presented on the end-papers of relevant books (see page 128).

The Nature series comprised twenty-five titles produced between 1953 and 1979. An expansive subject list included all types of birds as well as butterflies, moths and insects, pets, wild flowers and trees, the weather and the night sky. Few aspects of British nature were left untouched.

What to Look for in Winter
536 Nature, 1959.
Illustrations by
C. F. Tunnicliffe.

What to Look for in Spring
536 Nature, 1961.
Illustrations by
C. F. Tunnicliffe.

What to Look for in Winter, *What to Look for in Spring*, *What to Look for in Summer* and *What to Look for in Autumn* were also hugely popular titles in the Nature series. Illustrated by Charles Frederick Tunnicliffe, a much-respected and renowned naturalistic painter of birds and wildlife, the series encouraged the reader, through E. L. Grant Watson's text, to explore the British countryside with the book as their guide, noting that it would 'greatly increase the pleasure of your country walks'.

Other Ladybird series concerned with nature included Natural History (series 651), with nine titles sporadically released between 1965 and 1980, and Animals of the World (series 691), written and illustrated by John Leigh-Pemberton, which ventured beyond the shores of Great Britain to explore animals from across the globe.

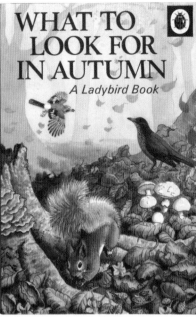

What to Look for in Summer
536 Nature, 1960.
Illustrations by
C. F. Tunnicliffe.

What to Look for in Autumn
536 Nature, 1960.
Illustrations by
C. F. Tunnicliffe.

The Conservation books (series 727), first published in 1972, showed an increasing awareness of environmental issues with titles including *Disappearing Mammals* and *What on Earth are We Doing?* The recent acknowledgement of a sustained threat to the natural environment had led Ladybird to take a conscientious stance in educating young readers to the realities of the relationship between Man and Nature. 'For too long Man has believed that he can dominate, exploit and alter Nature with impunity,' the introduction to *Wild Life in Britain* read, whilst *Disappearing Mammals* went further still: 'Man has no right to rob future generations of the interest, inspiration and beauty that can be had from contact with animals.'

What to Look for in Spring
536 Nature, 1961.
Illustrations by
C. F. Tunnicliffe.

Charles Tunnicliffe

Charles Frederick Tunnicliffe, born in Langley, near Macclesfield, in 1901, was an accomplished artist, best known for his paintings and prints depicting the wildlife of the British countryside. He trained at the Macclesfield School of Art and the Manchester School of Art before winning a scholarship to the Royal College of Art where he graduated with a diploma in painting.

Tunnicliffe was already an established and renowned artist when he was commissioned by Ladybird to create illustrations for *The Farm* and *What to Look for in Spring*, *What to Look for in Summer*, *What to Look for in Autumn* and *What to Look for in Winter*. All five titles became instant classics due to their beautifully illustrated images of the British countryside and their attention to detail.

Tunnicliffe's work was seen and known by millions during the 1950s and 1960s, not only through his work for Ladybird but also for his illustrations for Brooke Bond tea cards and Henry Williamson's *Tarka the Otter*. He was also commissioned to create cover illustrations for the Royal Society for the Protection of Birds

magazine and won the RSPB Gold Medal in 1975, just four years before his death in 1979.

Throughout his life, he explored many artistic mediums, creating captivating images using watercolours, oil paints, etching and aquatint, woodcut and wood engraving and scraperboard – all utilized to create memorable images of birds and animals in their natural settings.

What to Look for in Summer
536 Nature, 1960.
Illustrations by
C. F. Tunnicliffe.

What to Look for in Autumn
536 Nature, 1960.
Illustrations by
C. F. Tunnicliffe.

The water-vole in the foreground is squatting in shallow water by the canal-side, and is nibbling one of the many different kinds of leaves on which it feeds. The vole is a delicate feeder, and always keeps very clean even though it lives in a hole in a muddy bank. It must not be mistaken for a rat, as the vole has a broader forehead and much nicer habits. It is closely related to the short-tailed field-mouse, which is also a vole.

Two damsel-flies are on the tall, flowering rush. These are the smallest of the British dragon-flies, and they prey on gnats, July-browns and other insects. Beside the water-vole grow arrowhead plants, and to the left the great water-plantain. Both have three-petalled flowers. Their roots are deep in mud under the water, and they are growing in the shallows at the canal's edge together with the rushes. The canal passes under a bridge, and you can see how the tow-path also goes under it so that a horse that pulls a barge can pass thereon. On the towpath fishermen are sitting, and one of them has just caught a fish: not too big to be landed with a skilful jerk.

A kingfisher, like a streak of living sapphire, flashes across the water. He knows better than the fishermen how to catch fish. His whole interest is in little fish, and he and his wife make their nest out of fish-bones.

28

What to Look for in Summer
536 Nature, 1960.
Illustrations by
C. F. Tunnicliffe.

Wild Life in Britain
727 Conservation, 1972.
Illustrations by
John Leigh-Pemberton.

The original cover artwork
for *Wild Life in Britain*.

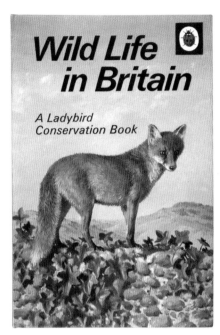

Disappearing Mammals
727 Conservation, 1973.
Cover illustration by
John Leigh-Pemberton.

What on Earth Are We Doing?
727 Conservation, 1976.
Illustrations by Pat Oakley.
The topic of conservation
was particularly close to
Douglas Keen's heart, and this
is the only Ladybird book in
which he is credited as a co-author.

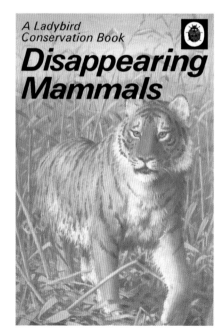

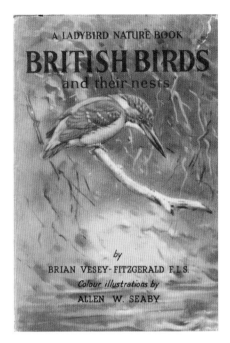

British Birds and their Nests
536 Nature, 1953.
Illustrations by Allen W. Seaby.

*A Second Book of British Birds
and their Nests*
536 Nature, 1953.
Illustrations by Allen W. Seaby.

The Blue Tit

This lovely little bird is very common in gardens and towns, and will eat almost anything. If you put out food on a bird table in your garden, the Blue Tits will come for it and soon get very tame; or when you hang up a lump of fat or a coconut, they will cling to it upside down to eat, and look very pretty

If you put up a nest box, the Blue Tits are almost certain to come and nest in your garden. They are also very fond of pecking off the caps of milk-bottles when left on the doorstep in the morning.

12

British Birds and their Nests
536 Nature, 1953.
Illustrations by Allen W. Seaby.

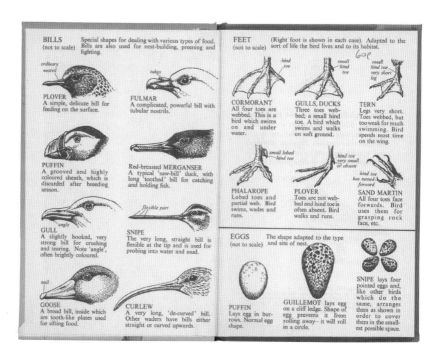

Ladybird by Design

Plants and How They Grow
651 Natural History, 1965.
Illustrations by Ronald Lampitt.

Life of the Honey-bee
651 Natural History, 1969.
Illustrations by J. Payne.

Adventures from History

Comprising forty-nine titles in total and published between 1956 and 1978, Adventures from History (series 561) was the largest Ladybird series and one of the most popular. As the introduction to the first title *King Alfred the Great* explained: 'This book tells you something of what England was like a thousand years ago.' The series examined numerous historical figures and, in the 1950s alone, introduced young readers to William the Conqueror, Sir Walter Raleigh, Nelson, Queen Elizabeth I, Captain Cook, Florence Nightingale and Julius Caesar.

The first twenty-three titles, published over eleven years until 1967, were all written by Lawrence du Garde Peach, a writer, dramatist and humourist, and illustrated by John Kenney, who was responsible for illustrating the Ladybird classic *Tootles the Taxi* amongst other titles. The combination of descriptive writing and distinctive artwork led to a very strong series that was exciting and informative.

The Adventures from History series brought history to life and was hugely popular with schoolchildren and teachers. The books provided an accessible route into the history of Britain, whilst also introducing readers to great civilizations of the world: the Aztecs, Mycenaeans, Vikings, Incas, Romans and Egyptians. Generations of young readers were inspired to learn more about the past through their early introduction to historical figures in Ladybird's series 561.

As the series title suggested, history was presented as a sequence of adventures and much was made of the lead figures' roles in shaping history. The protagonists of each title, given depth and personality by both author and illustrator, had their stories told boldly and descriptively and were illustrated with realism and attention to detail.

Atmospheric and dramatic, John Kenney's illustrative style was a suitable choice for the series. His depictions of battle scenes were action-packed and violent – but without a single drop of blood ever actually evident in the illustrations. Rarely was a title in the series published without the portrayal of a battle in full flow; the first ten in the series all featured dramatic fights, which were visually arresting and a compelling reason for any schoolchild to pick up a Ladybird Adventures from History book.

King Alfred the Great
561 Adventures from History,
1956. Illustrations by
John Kenney.

Julius Caesar and Roman Britain
561 Adventures from History, 1959. Illustrations by John Kenney.

William the Conqueror
561 Adventures from History, 1956. Illustrations by John Kenney.

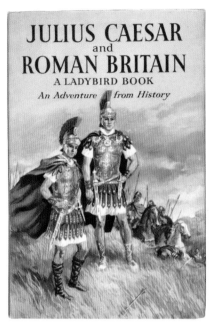

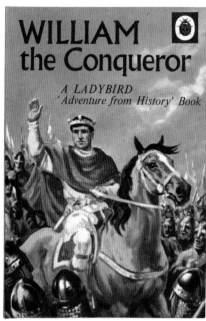

Florence Nightingale
561 Adventures from History, 1959. Illustrations by John Kenney.

Heroes and Heroines

From the defeat of the Spanish Armada by Sir Walter Raleigh and Admiral Lord Nelson's glory against the French at the Battle of Trafalgar to Captain Scott's voyage to the South Pole, the people in the Adventures from History series had exciting and brave lives. Leading women in history were also featured, including Queen Elizabeth I, Joan of Arc, Florence Nightingale and Cleopatra.

Ladybird by Design

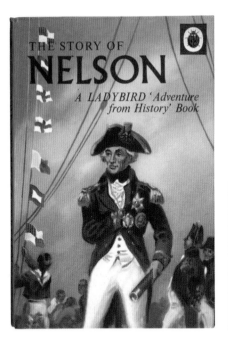

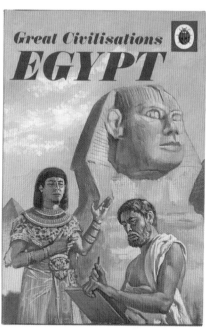

The Story of Nelson
561 Adventures from History,
1957. Illustrations
by John Kenney.

Great Civilisations: Egypt
561 Adventures from History,
1973. Illustrations by
Jorge Nuñez.

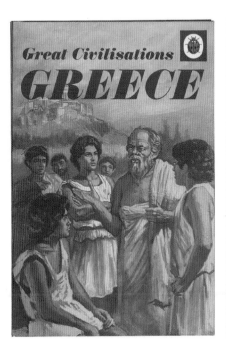

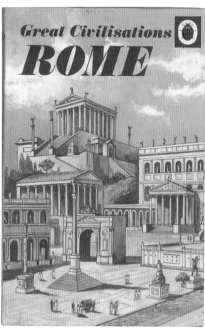

Great Civilisations: Greece
561 Adventures from History,
1974. Illustrations by
Jorge Nuñez.

Great Civilisations: Rome
561 Adventures from History,
1974. Illustrations by
Jorge Nuñez.

The Story of the First
Queen Elizabeth
561 Adventures from History,
1958. Illustrations
by John Kenney.

John Kenney

The illustrator of thirty-one Ladybird titles between 1954 and 1972, John Theodore Eardley Kenney was a prolific commercial artist and illustrator.

Born in 1911, Kenney studied at Leicester College of Art before serving with the 44th Searchlight Regiment and the 121st Light Anti-Aircraft Regiment during the Second World War, landing in Normandy on D-Day. Whilst not an official war artist, Kenney recorded the landings and his regiment's progress across Europe with drawings made on the spot.

After the war, Kenney returned to Leicester and worked at J. E. Slater, a company of commercial artists, until 1957, when he embarked upon a career as a full-time freelance illustrator.

Kenney's work for Ladybird spanned different series, including *The Silver Arrow – A Robin Hood Adventure* (series 549), *Tootles the Taxi* and *The Circus Comes to Town* (both series 413). Most famously, he created images for a great number of historical titles, such as *King Alfred the Great*, *The Pilgrim Fathers*, *Sir Walter Raleigh*, *The Story of Captain Cook*, *Charles Dickens* and *Florence Nightingale*.

Kenney's career was dogged by ill health and he lost sight in one eye in 1968. Despite this, and alongside his immense contribution to Ladybird, Kenney also illustrated Reverend Wilbert Awdry's Railway Series (which included *Thomas the Tank Engine*) between 1957 and 1962, following in the footsteps of Clarence Reginald Dalby, the first illustrator of the series.

Kenney died in 1972 at the age of sixty-one, leaving behind a timeless legacy of Ladybird books.

The Story of the First Queen Elizabeth 561 Adventures from History, 1958. Illustrations by John Kenney.

Frank Hampson

The illustrator behind *Kings and Queens of England, Book 1* and *Book 2* was Frank Hampson. He created illustrations for Ladybird over a six-year period from 1964, and also provided illustrations for *A First Book of Nursery Rhymes* (Fairy Tales and Rhymes series 413) and the subsequent two titles as well as two of the titles from the Key Words Reading Scheme (series 641).

Hampson's research was meticulous and carried out in the same manner for each book – family and friends, even the local milkman, were drafted in to pose as models for his characters.

Born in 1918 in Audenshaw, near Manchester, Hampson was a prolific artist from an early age. Entering a drawing competition run by *Meccano* magazine, he not only won a prize for his entry but also picked up a regular commission for the publication and by the age of thirteen he was working as a freelance illustrator and comic artist.

On leaving school, Hampson began working for the Post Office, creating illustrations for its official magazine *The Post*. Two years later, he left to study art at the Victoria College of Arts and Science in Southport. A year after his graduation, war broke out and Hampson saw active service in France and Belgium, the experience informing his work in later years.

After the war, Hampson worked as an illustrator for *The Anvil*, a Church of England magazine out of which the *Eagle* comic was born when its editor Reverend Marcus Morris had the idea of producing a high-quality comic presenting Christian values. The high calibre of the comic was a combination of Morris's determination and Hampson's mastery of storytelling through illustration. A meticulous draughtsman, Hampson is best known for creating the legendary comic character, Dan Dare.

In 1964, Hampson parted company with *Eagle* and joined Ladybird, his talents as an artist having been spotted by Douglas Keen. In 1970, a period of ill health saw Hampson leave Ladybird to work as a graphic design technician at Ewell Technical College and as a life-drawing tutor at Epsom School of Art. He died in 1985.

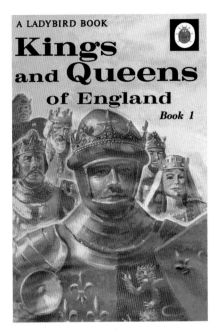

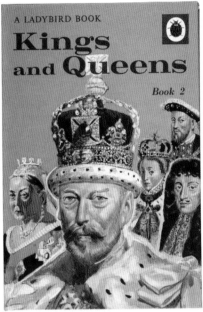

Kings and Queens of England Book 1
561 Adventures from History, 1968. Illustrations by Frank Hampson.

Kings and Queens Book 2
561 Adventures from History, 1968. Illustrations by Frank Hampson.

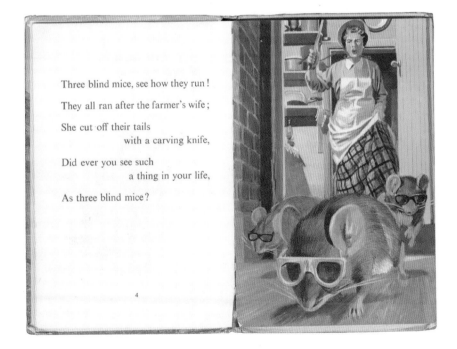

Three blind mice, see how they run!

They all ran after the farmer's wife;

She cut off their tails
       with a carving knife,

Did ever you see such
       a thing in your life,

As three blind mice?

4

A Third Ladybird Book of Nursery Rhymes
413 Fairy Tales and Rhymes, 1967. Illustrations by Frank Hampson.

Religion and Bible Stories

Christianity, Bible stories and prayers were to play a prominent role in Ladybird's output from the early 1950s through to the 1980s. The Ladybird emphasis on religion between these decades was predominantly focused on Christianity, as Britain for the most part remained a country dedicated to mainly Christian values and customs.

Ladybird's foray into publishing religious titles began with Bible Stories (series 522). *The Child of the Temple* was first published in 1952, with additional titles added to the series once or twice annually throughout the decade. These books, as the series title suggests, were a range of stories retold from the Bible, with the books published in the 1950s written by Lucy Diamond and illustrated by Kenneth Inns. Two later titles published in 1969 and 1970, *The Story of Saint Paul* and *The Story of Peter the Fisherman*, were written by D. S. Hare and illustrated by Eric Winter.

The Bible Stories books proved popular in Sunday schools throughout the UK and abroad. Inns's illustrations depicting characters and scenes from the Bible had a strikingly cinematic quality, possibly influenced by the great Hollywood blockbusters of the 1950s such as *The Robe* (1953), *Ben-Hur* (1959) and *The Ten Commandments* (1956). The Ladybird depiction of Jesus in *Jesus by the Sea of Galilee*, published in 1958, and in *Jesus Calls his Disciples* from 1959 is of a statuesque figure, calm and confident, a man at peace with his faith in God – but also with a certain movie-star aura. Joseph, too, in *The Story of Joseph* from 1955 appears ready to take to the stage with Inns's dramatic illustrations bringing a touch of glamour to the narrative – the portrait-shaped images appearing as if snapshots from a wider cinema-screen format.

Bible stories in the Easy Reading list (series 606A), which included nine titles published between 1960 and 1978, continued the theme of tales from the Bible but were aimed at young readers rather than Sunday school teachers or parents. The three titles of Prayers and Hymns (series 612) followed in 1961 and aimed to give context to popular and well-known prayers.

In a new departure for Ladybird, *Animals, Birds and Plants of the Bible* was published in 1964, the first title in Facts About the Bible (series 649), with the aim of providing information about the flora and fauna mentioned in the Bible. The next book, *Life in New Testament Times*,

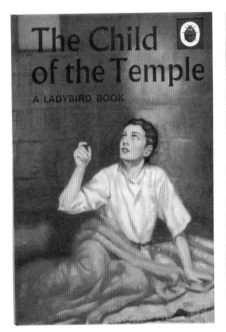

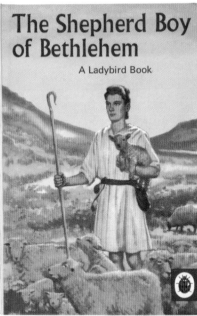

The Child of the Temple
522 Bible Stories, 1952.
Illustrations by Kenneth Inns.

The Shepherd Boy of Bethlehem
522 Bible Stories, 1953.
Illustrations by Kenneth Inns.

published in 1968, gave greater historical insights into the lives of people in Palestine during the time of the Old and New Testaments. *What to Look for Inside a Church* and *What to Look for Outside a Church*, both published in 1964, explored the meaning of and the reason behind objects inside a church and in a churchyard as illustrated reference guides.

From explaining the meaning of prayers and providing context for the lives of people in the Bible to looking at the significance of objects and elements within churches and churchyards and retelling well-known Bible stories, Ladybird's approach to the Christian religion was undeniably thorough.

The Lord's Prayer

The first title in Prayers and Hymns (series 612), *The Lord's Prayer and other prayers for children*, brilliantly illustrated by Harry Wingfield, gave context and meaning to the well-known prayers recited in schools and churches. Illustrations depict scenes such as a small boy helping an old man across a zebra crossing to demonstrate 'Thy will be done, as it is in heaven', and the same young boy touching the wet paint on a wall his father has just painted to explain 'and forgive us our trespasses'.

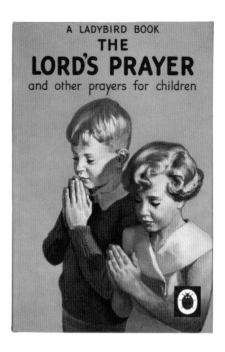

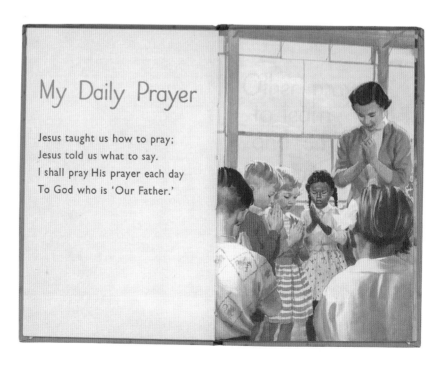

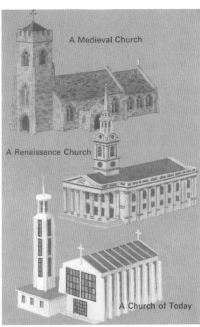

What to Look for Inside a Church
649 Facts About the Bible, 1972.
Illustrations by Ronald Lampitt.

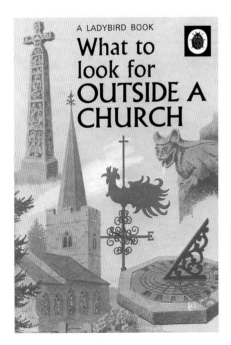

What to Look for Outside a Church
649 Facts About the Bible, 1972.
Illustrations by Ronald Lampitt.

What to Look for Inside a Church
649 Facts About the Bible, 1972.
Illustrations by Ronald Lampitt.

Stories About Children of the Bible
606A Bible Stories, 1962.
Illustrations by
Clive Uptton.

Jesus by the Sea of Galilee
522 Bible Stories, 1958.
Illustrations by Kenneth Inns.

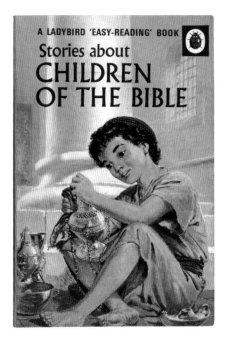

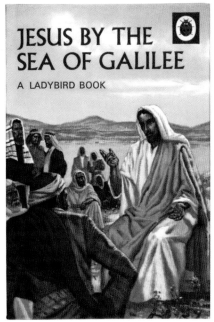

Jesus Calls his Disciples
522 Bible Stories, 1959.
Illustrations by Kenneth Inns.

Life in New Testament Times
649 Facts About the Bible, 1968.
Illustrations by Eric Winter.

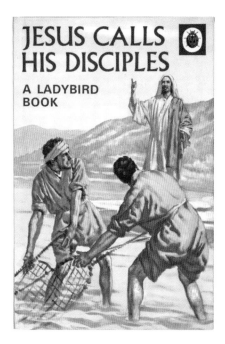

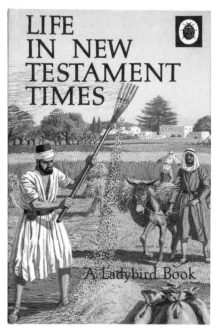

Ladybird by Design

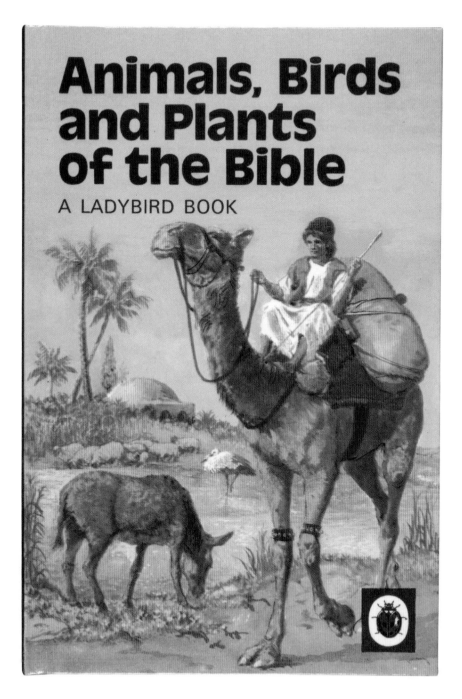

Animals, Birds and Plants of the Bible
649 Facts About the Bible, 1964.
Illustrations by Clive Uptton.

Ladybird by Design

Achievements

The start of the 1960s was a turning point for Ladybird, with the proliferation of non-fiction titles and the launch of many new series. During the 1960s, twenty-eight new series were launched – twenty more than the previous decade. With a greater emphasis on factual titles, Ladybird books encouraged children to learn more about the world around them, albeit often from a very British perspective.

Achievements (series 601), launched in 1960, aimed to inspire young readers with information and stories about how humankind's accomplishments had helped shape the modern world. The first title, *The Story of Flight,* focused on Britain's contribution to aviation, celebrating landmark aircraft and the pilots who flew them. Further championing of Britain's contribution to humankind was evident in the third publication of the series, *The Story of Railways*: 'Great Britain has led the world in nearly every aspect of railway development,' offered author Richard Bowood. The book concentrated on George Stephenson's steam locomotive *Rocket* as well as the launch of the first city underground line in London in 1863. The evidence presented was clear – Britain was the protagonist of humankind's achievements.

A good proportion of the first titles to appear in the Achievements series were written by Richard Bowood (the pen name of David Scott Daniell) and illustrated by Robert Ayton. Ayton was very clearly a firm favourite at Ladybird: the introduction to *The Story of Railways*, published in 1961, described the book as 'magnificently illustrated by Robert Ayton', whilst the blurb from *The Story of Houses and Homes*, published in 1963, described his artwork as 'superb even by Ladybird standards!'

Robert Ayton's artworks for *The Story of Our Churches and Cathedrals*, published in 1964, went one step further than previous contributions: a set of black-and-white diagrammatic drawings appeared on each page alongside the text. Ayton's work for *The Story of Radio* demonstrated his versatility further still with the creation of scientific images and infographics, as well as his more traditional scenic illustrations.

The Story of Flight
601 Achievements, 1960.
Illustrations by Robert Ayton.

The Story of Railways
601 Achievements, 1961.
Illustrations by Robert Ayton.

However, the achievements of humankind were not solely confined to those occurring in Great Britain – or even on Earth. *Exploring Space*, first published in 1964, could only speculate on the space race and whether a journey to the moon might one day be a reality. Written by Roy Worvill and illustrated by B. Knight, *Exploring Space* was later updated to cover the moon landing of 21 July 1969, with additional illustrations created by B. H. Robinson. Ladybird, committed to ensuring that their books remained current and relevant, would often update titles rather than simply reprint them.

No stone was left unturned for the Achievements series – from space and underwater exploration to general scientific discoveries with *The Story of Science Book 1* and *Book 2*, and more specific achievements with, for example, *The Story of Medicine* and *The Story of Nuclear Power*. Metals, plastics, radio, printing and newspapers were all covered as the series expanded to twenty-seven titles in total.

Popular and accessible, the Achievements series celebrated the success of humankind in a positive and engaging way, indicative of Ladybird's approach to publishing.

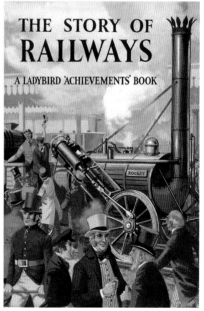

Exploring Space (first edition)
601 Achievements, 1964.
Illustrations by B. Knight.

Exploring Space (revised edition),
601 Achievements, 1972.
Illustrations by B. Knight and
B. H. Robinson.

How Much do We Weigh?

You have probably read about Sir Isaac Newton, and how he saw a falling apple and linked it up with the worlds in space through the law of gravity. This acts as though the earth were a great magnet which pulls things towards it. But we must think of the magnet as though it were not on the surface of the earth where we live, but buried deep at the centre, four thousand miles beneath our feet. Since the earth is not quite a sphere, but bulges round the equator and is slightly flattened at the poles, we are farther from the magnet at the equator than we are at the poles, and so we weigh a little less on the equator.

If we get four thousand miles from the earth's surface an object would weigh only a quarter of its normal weight. A man who weighs seventy two kilograms would weigh only eighteen kilograms at the same distance. On the moon, where the gravity pull is only one sixth of that of the earth, the same man would weigh no more than twelve kilograms.

As we have already seen, the space-traveller who is going up in a rocket will weigh three or four times more than normal, the exact increase depending on how quickly the rocket is accelerating. The men who have circled the earth in a space-craft have first experienced this great increase in weight and then the complete opposite. Once in orbit they become weightless, because the speed of their space-craft as it circles the earth tends to throw them outwards, and this just cancels out the pull of the earth's gravity.

34   *An astronaut floats without weight*

Exploring Space (first edition)
601 Achievements, 1964.
Illustrations by B. Knight.

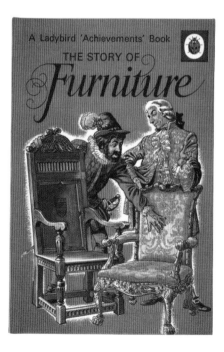

Robert Ayton

Born in London in 1915 and educated at the Harrow School of Art, Robert Ayton worked as a commercial artist for several advertising agencies. His clients included Rolls-Royce and Castrol. After serving in the Second World War, Ayton returned to work as a freelance illustrator.

Later, Ayton worked for the comic *Eagle*, drawing Jack O'Lantern for nine years. He then worked briefly for the comic *Girl*, before returning to *Eagle* to draw *The Golden Man*, a biography of Sir Walter Raleigh. He was first commissioned by Ladybird in 1960 to provide the illustrations for *The Story of Flight* (series 601). Ayton went on to illustrate fifty titles in total for Ladybird, creating images for a diverse range of subjects with accuracy and attention to detail. His books include: *The Story of Furniture*, *Great Inventions* and *The Story of Railways* (all series 601); *The Ladybird Book of the Weather* (series 536), and *The Ladybird Book of Toys and Games to Make* (series 633).

Ayton later taught illustration at the University of the West of England and joined an artistic group called the Bristol Savages before his death in 1985 at the age of seventy.

The Story of Metals
601 Achievements, 1971.
Illustrations by
Martin Aitchison.

The Story of Plastics
601 Achievements, 1972.
Illustrations by
B. H. Robinson.

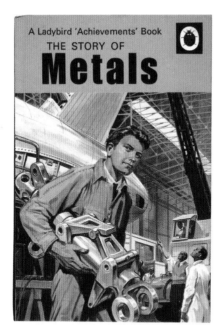

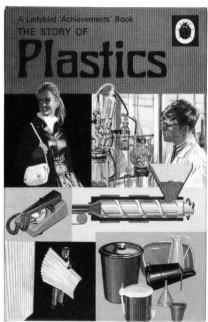

The Story of Nuclear Power
601 Achievements, 1972.
Illustrations by
Robert Ayton.

The Story of Medicine
601 Achievements, 1972.
Illustrations by
Robert Ayton.

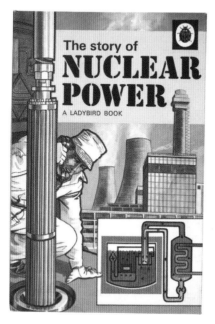

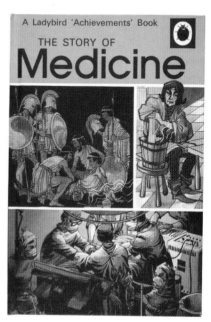

Diagrams

The presentation of scientific or technical facts and specifications was key to many Ladybird titles. Douglas Keen's vision that Ladybird books should be both educational and enjoyable ensured that the illustrators were briefed to make diagrams and charts (today widely referred to as infographics) accessible and easy to understand. Previously books containing factual charts had presented the information in dry and monochromatic ways. The best Ladybird diagrams were educational, informative and useful, but also visually arresting. They were used to give the reader information in a more digestible format than could be portrayed in the text, such as presenting cross-sections of planets in the Solar System, demonstrating the scale or height of man-made structures, or showing weight or volume.

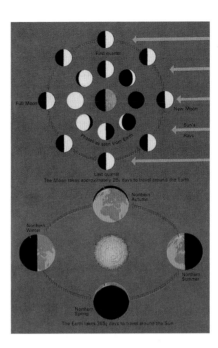

The Story of Science Book 1
601 Achievements, 1973.
Illustrations by
B. H. Robinson.

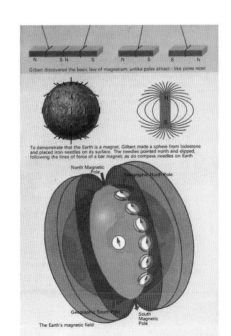

The Story of Science Book 2
601 Achievements, 1973.
Illustrations by
B. H. Robinson.

People at Work

Between 1962 and 1973, when the twenty titles in People at Work (series 606B) were first published, Britain was a rapidly changing country. Widespread social changes were taking place; class divisions were beginning to be dismantled after the end of the Second World War, and a sense of freedom and optimism was finally returning after the austerity of the 1950s.

People at Work (series 606B) reflected traditional employment during the 1960s and early 1970s and today provides an intriguing snapshot of British industry during an era of industrial prosperity, when building and manufacturing were thriving. This was an age – pre-digital of course – when Britain's workforce was mainly engaged in manual labour. *The Builder*, *The Miner*, *The Shipbuilders* and *The Pottery Makers* all reflected the very hands-on and practical nature of work. A sense of Britain's future and the reliance we would eventually place on the car and road transportation can also be seen in *The Road Makers* as a vision for Britain's network of motorways unfolded.

The series was entirely illustrated by John Berry, a war artist before his twenty-year career working for Ladybird. His artwork captured the essence of British working life, albeit from a mostly male perspective. At a time when men and women still had very defined, stereotypical gender roles, women seldom feature in the series, and where they do we are reminded of their supporting role. In *The Nurse* we learn that 'the doctors tell nurses what to do', and in *The Customs Officer* if female customs officers 'are not busy, they help with the office work'. Only in *The Policeman* do we learn that 'policewomen are trained in the same way as the men and they can do the same jobs. They arrest criminals, just as policemen do.'

Berry's illustrations, drawn from his own photographic reference material and sketches he made watching people at work, sensitively captured real-life scenarios. Rather mundane situations appear almost frozen in time – from the images of draughtsmen working in an office in *The Road Makers* to men mail-sorting in *The Postman and the Postal Service* or plastering walls in *The Builder*, it is the everyday aspects of each career that today offer such fascinating insights into Britain's workforce during the 1960s and 1970s.

The Policeman
606B People at Work, 1962.
Illustrations by John Berry.

Brave and Exciting Work

The Fireman
606B People at Work, 1962.
Illustrations by John Berry.

Acting as mini career guides, the People at Work titles that cover the emergency services (*The Fireman, The Policeman* and *The Life-boat Men*) and the armed forces (*The Soldier, The Sailor* and *The Airman in the Royal Air Force*) impart a sense of heroism to these roles. The 'important and brave work' of life-boat men is celebrated, and 'interesting and accurate information' about the army is given. For Ladybird's young readers, particularly young boys, a career in these areas must have appeared incredibly adventurous and exciting.

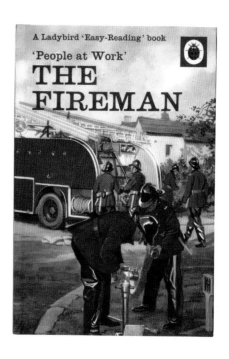

The Soldier
606B People at Work, 1966.
Illustrations by John Berry.

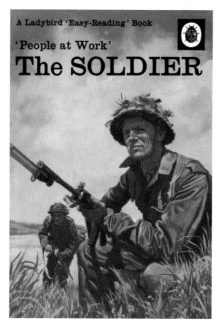

The Fireman
606B People at Work, 1962.
Original artwork by John Berry.

The Road Makers
606B People at Work, 1967.
Illustrations by John Berry.

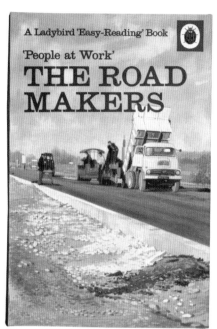

The Pottery Makers
606B People at Work, 1969.
Illustrations by John Berry.

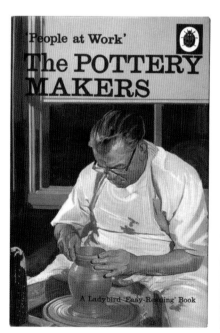

On the Railways
606B People at Work, 1972.
Illustrations by John Berry.

The Postman and the Postal Service
606B People at Work, 1965.
Illustrations by John Berry.

The Car Makers
606B People at Work, 1968.
Illustrations by John Berry.

John Berry

Between 1961 and 1978, John Berry created the illustrations for twenty-five Ladybird books, including the memorable People at Work series (606B).

Born in Hammersmith, London, in 1920, Berry trained at Hammersmith College of Art before being offered a scholarship at the Royal Academy, which he chose not to take up, instead enlisting in the RAF at the outbreak of the Second World War. Sent to the Middle East, Berry offered to design and illustrate a poster advertising a national day of prayer. The poster was spotted by Air Marshal Arthur Tedder who promptly seconded Berry as a war artist in the Eighth Army in the Western Desert. It was a source of pride for Berry was that he was the only war artist taken from the ranks, with some of his artworks exhibited during wartime at the National Gallery in London. These are now in the permanent collection of the Imperial War Museum.

Following the end of the war, Berry started illustrating children's books and began to paint portraits on commission. He also freelanced for advertising agencies, including drawing the Esso tiger for ten years. He came up with the famous campaign copy-line 'Put a tiger in your tank', for which he was paid a flat fee of just £25 (a story he very much liked recounting).

Commissioned to work for Ladybird by Douglas Keen, the visionary editorial director, his first task was to illustrate *The Ladybird Book of London* (series 618). For fun he placed his own two-tone Ford estate car in front of the Bank of England. As well as illustrating the entire People at Work series and contributing to the Key Words Reading Scheme, Berry also illustrated Ladybird's *Hannibal the Hamster* titles (part of series 497) and the Visiting Countries books (series 606G). Thereafter he returned to portraiture, with President George Bush Senior and Diana, Princess of Wales, amongst his subjects. Berry died in December 2009 at the age of eighty-nine.

The City

A short bus ride, or an interesting walk, will take us to the Monument, in Fish Street. The Monument is a fluted column two hundred and two feet high, with a gilded device at the top representing flames. It was built in 1677 to commemorate the Great Fire of London of 1666, which began in a baker's shop exactly two hundred and two feet away, in Pudding Lane.

There are three hundred and eleven steps inside the Monument, and if you do not mind getting puffed, climb to the top; the view over London is wonderful.

Another short bus ride takes us through the busy streets of offices to the Mansion House, the official home of the Lord Mayor of London. Stand outside the Mansion House and look around you, for this is the very heart of the City.

Standing proudly on its island is the Royal Exchange, and its steps are another place from which a new Sovereign is proclaimed. Across the road is the Bank of England, a massive and, naturally enough, very safe-looking building.

This busy, bustling home of banks and offices has its roots deep in the history of old London. Once rich merchants lived here, and high-spirited young apprentices slept under the counters, and sallied forth eagerly when the cry "Out Clubs!" was raised, the cry calling the apprentices to fight. In this city a boy named Dick once began his career which ended with him being Sir Richard Whittington, thrice Lord Mayor of London.

28   **The Royal Exchange**

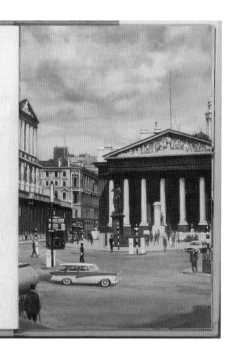

The Ladybird Book of London
618 Capital Cities of the World, 1961. Illustrations by John Berry.

When the ambulance arrives after an accident, the ambulance men lift the injured person on to a stretcher. Then they slide the stretcher gently into the ambulance.

One ambulance man, or a nurse, sits in the van beside the injured person.

The driver then drives to hospital as quickly as he can. He can use his bell or his flashing light to tell other traffic to keep out of the way.

28

The Nurse
606B People at Work, 1963. Illustrations by John Berry.

The Public Services

The Public Services (series 606E) was a short series of just three titles: *Electricity* published in 1966, *Gas* in 1967 and *Water Supply* in 1969. Each title, aimed at young readers and subtitled 'A Ladybird "Easy-Reading" book', used 'simple, clear text and excellent, full-colour illustrations', and was written by the husband-and-wife team of I. and J. Havenhand. It was illustrated by the artist John Berry, also known for the People at Work series.

Part public information, part science and engineering, the Public Services books aimed to demystify the processes involved in providing homes and businesses with electricity, gas and water in easily comprehensible language. Brought to life with illustrations by John Berry spanning the historical, the scientific and the technical, the images were both informative and atmospheric.

Many of the complexities of the technical processes involved in large-scale gas-fields, electricity sub-stations, dams and reservoirs were visually explained through Berry's fascinating diagrams. Young readers were encouraged to grasp difficult concepts through accurate cut-away diagrams, maps and annotated images, which all played their part in bringing the narrative to life.

The Public Services series educated its readers by conveying complex subject matter in a simple way, using a tone of voice that was authoritative, without being condescending or patronizing. The illustrations also enabled the reader to engage with the subject matter in an adult way. The intended audience was, of course, a young one, but the presentation of the text and images ensured that these books were not simply dismissed as children's books. One of the titles was even utilized by the industry it featured: a special edition of *Water Supply* was published for the Yorkshire Water Authority to accompany its educational programmes for schools.

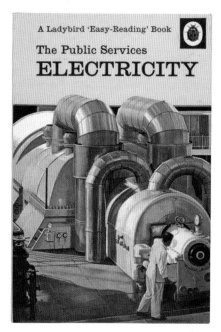

Electricity
606E The Public Services, 1966.
Illustrations by John Berry.

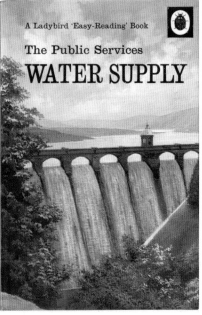

Gas
606E The Public Services, 1967.
Illustrations by John Berry.

Water Supply
606E The Public Services, 1969.
Illustrations by John Berry.

Each book began by exploring the history of each service. *Gas* covered the discovery by William Murdoch in the 1790s that gas flames could be ignited to emit light, and *Electricity* the discovery by Michael Faraday in 1831 that electricity could be passed through a wire. Berry's illustrations bring the past to life with great detail: Faraday in his laboratory is depicted with as much realism as the book's later illustrations, many created using photographic references.

Hydro means water, and so electricity made by water power is made at Hydro-electric Power Stations.

A dam is made across a valley and this holds back the water and stores it in a reservoir. The water can be used at any time. It flows through very large pipes to the power station, built near the bottom of the dam.

The water turns wheels built into the ends of the pipes. These are called water turbines and they drive the electric generators.

16

TURBINE TURNED BY WATER
WORKS THE ELECTRIC GENERATOR

Electricity
606E The Public Services, 1966.
Illustrations by John Berry.

The water is pumped through pipes from the reservoir to the city that owns it. The distance from a dam to a city may be as much as seventy miles.

If the water comes from a distant reservoir or river, it is pumped up, or can flow down, to tanks or storage reservoirs near the cities, towns or villages. The water stands in the storage reservoirs for a while.

While it is standing, any dirt in the water settles to the bottom. Some germs are killed by sunshine, and the wind helps to take away any nasty taste or smell that the water may have.

30

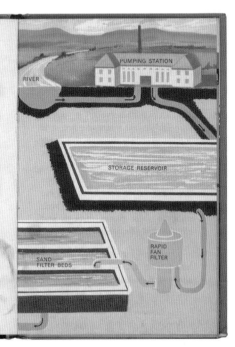

RIVER
PUMPING STATION
STORAGE RESERVOIR
RAPID FAN FILTER
SAND FILTER BEDS

Water Supply
606E The Public Services, 1969.
Illustrations by John Berry.

Visiting Countries

Travel for the average family during the early era of Ladybird books meant visiting the British coast during the summer holidays, in the family car, by train or by coach. European holidays were considered an extravagance, and with so much in Great Britain to see and explore – our countryside and wildlife, history and heritage – foreign travel was deemed both unaffordable and unnecessary.

By the mid-1970s much was to change. With an explosion of cheap package holidays to the continent, many of Britain's youth experienced their first holidays abroad, an encounter that their parents probably would not have undergone at a similar age. For the first time European, and latterly global, travel was to be increasingly the norm for family holidays and weekend breaks.

Ladybird's world, very firmly situated in and primarily reflecting upon Great Britain, was also to embrace European and worldwide travel much more openly. Where travel in its books had been previously confined to the historical tales of great discovery by famous explorers, such as Captain Cook, Sir Walter Raleigh and Christopher Columbus in Adventures from History (series 561), by 1969 the premise of Visiting Countries (series 606G) was that Great Britain's children might be interested in learning more about our European neighbours.

Come to France, the first title in the series, written by Irene Dark and beautifully illustrated by John Berry, opens with an introduction almost hesitant in tone: 'This book gives an interesting and colourful glimpse of a lovely country and her people. It shows some of the exciting things you might see if you go to France, and some of the differences in the way of life of the French people compared with your own.' Ladybird acknowledged travel to foreign places was not yet the norm, but if it were undertaken it was to be an educational experience and could be related to life at home in the UK. With just another two titles, *Come to Denmark* and *Come to Holland*, both published in 1971, the series was surprisingly short-lived.

Come to France
606G Visiting Countries,
1969. Illustrations
by John Berry.

II. A Design for Life

Come to France
606G Visiting Countries,
1969. Illustrations
by John Berry.

Come to Holland
606G Visiting Countries,
1971. Illustrations
by John Berry.

Come to Denmark
606G Visiting Countries,
1971. Illustrations
by John Berry.

Ladybird by Design

Bicycle racing is a well-loved sport in France. There are many local races, but for most French people the most important event is the 'Tour de France'. This race lasts for twenty to twenty-five days in summer. Racers come from all over the world to compete. They have to ride along the roads that go all round the edge of France. They have to pedal along under scorching skies, and climb mountain passes hundreds of metres high. They face the risk of many accidents, such as being bumped by another racer or even falling down cliffs.

An ambulance helicopter follows the race in case of such accidents. At the end of each 'lap' the riders sleep in the town they have reached.

The next morning everyone turns out to cheer them on their way. The race ends in Paris amid great excitement.

50

Come to France
606G Visiting Countries, 1969. Illustrations by John Berry.

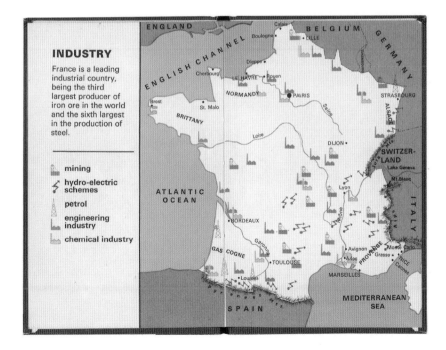

INDUSTRY

France is a leading industrial country, being the third largest producer of iron ore in the world and the sixth largest in the production of steel.

mining
hydro-electric schemes
petrol
engineering industry
chemical industry

Come to France
606G Visiting Countries, 1969. End-paper by John Berry.

Travel

Flight One Australia
587 Travel, 1958.
Illustrations by
Jack Matthew.

Travel (series 587) was a successful venture for Ladybird. The places visited were viewed through the eyes of brother and sister Alison and John, who were fortunate enough to travel the world with their father – they were perhaps a more grown-up version of Peter and Jane, with an inquisitive nature and an appetite for travel that knew no bounds. Between 1958 and 1962, Alison and John flew to Australia, Canada, the USA, India, Africa and the Holy Land.

The books were written by David Scott Daniell, who wrote numerous Ladybird titles under the name Richard Bowood. They were

Flight Four India
587 Travel, 1960.
Illustrations by
Jack Matthew.

illustrated by Jack Matthew, a versatile artist also known for his illustration work for *The Story of Football* and *The Story of Cricket* (series 606C). Matthew brilliantly captured the essence of each geographic location, covering landscape, history, wildlife and people. Whilst Peter and Jane were depicted in almost every illustration in Key Words, we see Alison and John's travels entirely through their eyes: across the six books and a total of 144 illustrations the reader never actually comes face to face with the intrepid siblings.

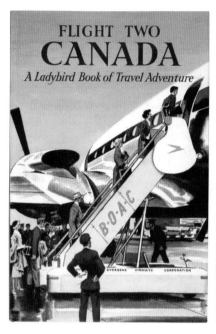

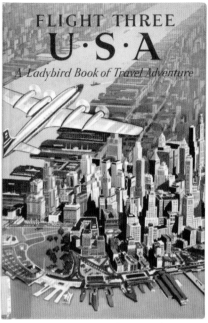

Flight Two Canada
587 Travel, 1959.
Illustrations by Jack Matthew.

Flight Three USA
587 Travel, 1959.
Illustrations by Jack Matthew.

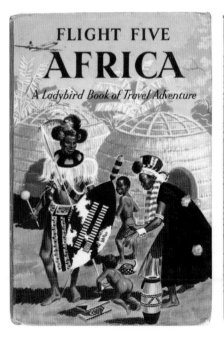

Flight Five Africa
587 Travel, 1961.
Illustrations by Jack Matthew.

Flight Six The Holy Land
587 Travel, 1962.
Illustrations by Jack Matthew.

Flight Three USA
587 Travel, 1959.
Illustrations by
Jack Matthew.

Ladybird by Design

Flight Three USA
587 Travel, 1959.
Illustrations by
Jack Matthew.

Flight One Australia
587 Travel, 1958.
Illustrations by
Jack Matthew.

Flight Six The Holy Land
587 Travel, 1962.
Illustrations by
Jack Matthew.

Flight Four India
587 Travel, 1960.
Illustrations by
Jack Matthew.

Flight Two Canada
587 Travel, 1959.
Illustrations by
Jack Matthew.

Indigenous People

Ladybird's portrayal of the wider world up until the 1970s was one that chimed with the views and thoughts of most people in Britain at the time. Whilst with the benefit of hindsight we might be tempted to re-enter Ladybird's world and critique the values of the day through the lens of the 21st century, it is worth remembering that just a few decades ago information on and empathy towards different cultures was not widely known. Britain's understanding of the world in the early 1960s was still resolutely based upon the notion of the British Empire. The portrayal of the indigenous people in Ladybird's world therefore relied on representations drawn from films and adventure books rather than photographic reference, and did little to offer any deep under-standing of the vital and interesting cultural differences between the reader, who was most likely British, and the reader's counter-parts in Africa, North and South America or the Middle East.

Flight One Australia
587 Travel, 1958.
Illustrations by
Jack Matthew.

Junior Science

What is air? Why does an astronaut wear a special suit? What is white light? These are just a few of the questions posed, and answered, in Junior Science (series 621). With just four books in the series – *Magnets, Bulbs and Batteries* and *Light, Mirrors and Lenses* (both published in 1962), and *Air, Wind and Flight* and *Levers, Pulleys and Engines* (published the following year) – it was nevertheless a successful series, reprinted many times throughout the 1970s.

All four books were written by Frank Edward Newing and Richard Bowood (the pen name for David Scott Daniell, who was a prolific writer of children's books and radio plays), and were created for young children as an introduction to science and scientific understanding. The books were illustrated by J. H. Wingfield, probably best known for his illustrations of Peter and Jane in the Key Words Reading Scheme.

Harry Wingfield's illustrations depict young boys and girls (in *Magnets, Bulbs and Batteries* the duo are based on his son and Douglas Keen's daughter, Caroline), conducting experiments at home. Only occasionally under the watchful eye of an adult, both children are energetically utilizing household objects to discover how magnets work, how electricity is conducted or how lenses reflect light.

By today's standards, much of what this series encouraged children to do would be deemed beyond the norms of basic health and safety. Children are shown using a magnifying glass to scorch paper in order to light a campfire in *Light, Mirrors and Lenses,* whilst another duo are instructed to take batteries apart; 'tear off some of the zinc-casing of one of the cells with a pair of pliers,' explains the text, whilst the accompanying illustration depicts the young girl grappling with said pliers and stripping back sharp metal battery casings. Children were encouraged to explore science through proactive engagement and whilst the risks were minimal, it is unthinkable that any children's book publisher today would consider promoting activities in the same way.

Despite the dangers, the books demonstrated that many projects could be undertaken at home on a rainy Sunday with a selection of objects and materials found around the house. They showed that the sciences could be fun for both boys and girls, that there were lots of fascinating activities that would enhance knowledge and understanding, and that a little risk might be just the thing to engage a junior scientist.

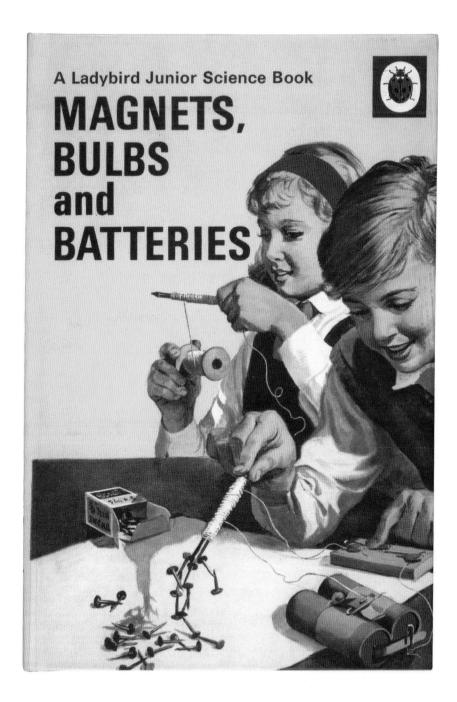

A Ladybird Junior Science Book

MAGNETS, BULBS and BATTERIES

Magnets, Bulbs and Batteries
621 Junior Science, 1962.
Illustrations by J. H. Wingfield.

Experiments at Home

Magnets, Bulbs and Batteries
621 Junior Science, 1962.
Illustrations by J. H. Wingfield.

Air, Wind and Flight
621 Junior Science, 1963.
Illustrations by J. H. Wingfield.

In an illustration from *Magnets, Bulbs and Batteries*, we see a boy placing his tongue between a strip of zinc and a carbon rod to create an electric current – 'you will feel a faint tickling'. Another young boy, this time in *Air, Wind and Flight*, is seen brandishing a penknife and carving a propeller from a block of soft wood. The text informs him to ensure he is 'always cutting away from himself' – the illustration shows him doing just so . . . but in the direction of another pair of young hands!

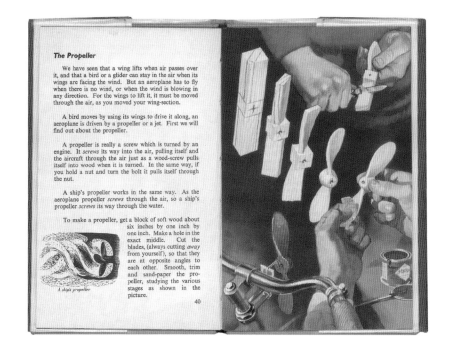

The Propeller

We have seen that a wing lifts when air passes over it, and that a bird or a glider can stay in the air when its wings are facing the wind. But an aeroplane has to fly when there is no wind, or when the wind is blowing in any direction. For the wings to lift it, it must be moved through the air, as you moved your wing-section.

A bird moves by using its wings to drive it along, an aeroplane is driven by a propeller or a jet. First we will find out about the propeller.

A propeller is really a screw which is turned by an engine. It *screws* its way into the air, pulling itself and the aircraft through the air just as a wood-screw pulls itself into wood when it is turned. In the same way, if you hold a nut and turn the bolt it pulls itself through the nut.

A ship's propeller works in the same way. As the aeroplane propeller *screws* through the air, so a ship's propeller *screws* its way through the water.

To make a propeller, get a block of soft wood about six inches by one inch by one inch. Make a hole in the exact middle. Cut the blades, (always cutting *away* from yourself), so that they are at opposite angles to each other. Smooth, trim and sand-paper the propeller, studying the various stages as shown in the picture.

A ship's propeller

40

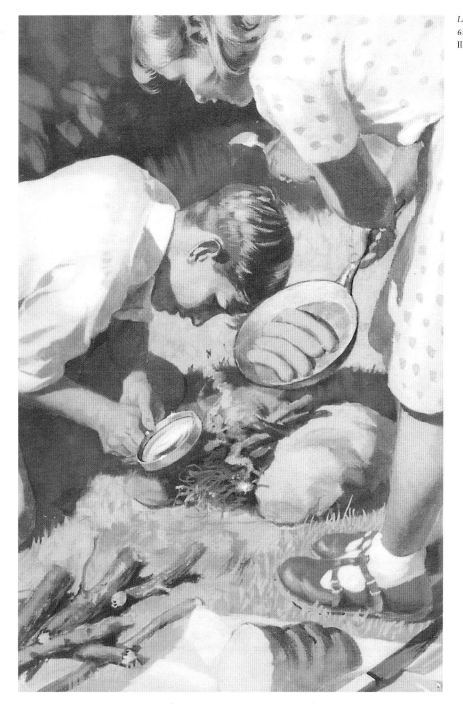

Light, Mirrors and Lenses
621 Junior Science, 1962.
Illustrations by J. H. Wingfield.

BOTH PAGES:
Light, Mirrors and Lenses
621 Junior Science, 1962.
Illustrations by J. H. Wingfield.

A Ladybird Junior Science Book

LIGHT, MIRRORS and LENSES

Making a Pinhole Camera

A pinhole camera works because light travels in straight lines.

To make a simple pinhole camera you need an empty tin, a piece of tissue (or greaseproof) paper and some thick brown paper. Cut out the closed end of the tin, and stick tissue paper over one open end and brown paper over the other. Make a pinhole in the middle of the brown paper—and there is your pinhole camera.

Hold it with the hole towards the window, cover your head and the tissue paper end of the tin with a dark cloth, and you should see a picture of the window. The picture you see will be upside down because the rays of light travelling in straight lines from the top and bottom of the window will have crossed as they pass through the pinhole. The diagram at the side shows how this happens.

To make a better pinhole camera you need two cardboard boxes which slide into each other. A box with a deep lid is ideal. Cut out a square from the bottom of the box and cover with brown paper. Then cut off the opposite end of the lid, and cover it completely with tissue paper. Make your pinhole in the brown paper as before.

You will again need to cover your head and the tissue paper end with a dark cloth. You can change the size of the picture by sliding one box into the other. The cloth

over your head is necessary because very little light comes through the pinhole, and the picture is not very bright. See what happens if you make more than one pinhole, or if you make a large pinhole.

10

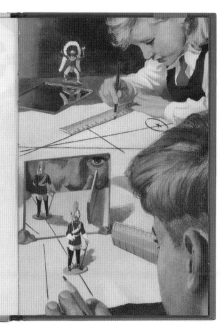

Through the Looking-glass

Stand in front of a wardrobe mirror and look at the carpet. You will see exactly the same amount of carpet-pattern between the image of your feet and the mirror as there is between your feet and the mirror. This shows that your image is as far behind the mirror as you are in front of it. You can find where an image is by a simple experiment.

Put a sheet of white paper on the table, and set up a mirror in the middle with plasticine. Stand a tin soldier or something small about six inches in front of the mirror. Make sure that there is as much paper behind the mirror as in front.

Lay a ruler on the paper pointing towards the mirror. Kneel down, and looking along the edge of the ruler move it until it points straight at the image, just as if the ruler is a rifle you are aiming at the image of the soldier. When your aim is exactly right, hold the ruler firmly and draw a line along the edge right up to the mirror.

Aim at the soldier's image from several other points, until you have three or four lines ruled on the paper, all pointing to the mirror. Rule a line on the paper where the mirror is standing and draw a ring where the soldier is standing. Take away the mirror and the soldier.

Continue the lines with the ruler until they meet behind the line where the mirror was. This is the point where you saw the image of the soldier. Measure the distance from the mirror to the spot where the soldier stood, and to the spot where the image was. These distances should be the same.

16

Hobbies and Interests

The Ladybird series Hobbies and Interests (series 633) and Learnabout (series 634) were aimed at the practically minded reader with titles introducing children to various crafts and hobbies in a simple yet engaging way. Fifty-four titles were published over seventeen years – Hobbies and Interests from 1963 to 1979, and Learnabout from 1967 to 1980.

Primarily focused on indoor activities, Hobbies and Interests encouraged children to pursue and enjoy a pastime or a craft, such as collecting stamps or coins, making puppets or dolls, knitting, sewing or crochet. This was of course well before the age of limitless children's television programmes, gaming consoles and the allure of the digital.

The titles presented positive and wholesome entertainment – the kind of activities that required concentration and hobbies that were good for mind, body and soul. Despite the overarching themes, there was very little sense of cohesion in terms of design across the two series. Robert Ayton's illustrations for *Toys and Games to Make*, first published in 1966 and the second title in the Hobbies and Interests series, look and feel very different to those by Bernard Herbert Robinson for *Indoor Gardening*, the next title in the series, which was published three years later.

Ayton's illustrations depict children enjoying themselves and making and playing with the toys they are creating; the books are clearly aimed at young readers in the Ladybird tradition. Robinson's images, however, appear far more grounded in natural history illustration and could very easily have been created for a book aimed at adults.

The third book in the series, *Stamp Collecting*, published in the same year as *Indoor Gardening*, understandably took a different design stance again. Stamps were reproduced at almost their original size, laid out on the page in a manner closely resembling a stamp album.

Where illustrators had previously been briefed to keep a consistent illustrative approach, in this series there was much more flexibility. Robinson's illustrations for *Coarse Fishing*, first published in 1969, show children happily engaged in activities and pursuits, the first artwork in the book being of a beaming young angler having landed his first big catch.

Stamps and land transport

All forms of land transport have always been popular subjects for stamps, both among the authorities issuing them and among collectors. Once again, we can illustrate only a selection.

The special delivery stamp from the United States shows a motor cycle dating from 1922, while the next stamp from Great Britain features a number of Minis and an 'E' type Jaguar car. The diamond-shaped stamp from Hungary shows an exciting scene from sidecar racing. The next stamp, also from Hungary, illustrates an articulated trolley-bus in Budapest, while the parcel post stamp from Bulgaria features a motor-cycle combination used for delivery purposes. On the Russian stamp we can see a scene from a cycle race, while the last stamp, again from the United States, was issued as part of a campaign to stop road accidents. It bears the inscription 'enforcement, education, engineering', these being the three most important factors in the prevention of road accidents.

14   *Cycles, motor cycles, cars and road safety.*

UNITED STATES

GREAT BRITAIN

HUNGARY

RUSSIA

BULGARIA

UNITED STATES

A Ladybird Book About
Stamp Collecting
633 Hobbies and Interests, 1969.
Written by Ian F. Finlay.

The stamps are mostly taken from the author's own collection.

Pips into plants

It is great fun to grow fruit pips, stones and seeds from trees, etc. An acorn will grow if balanced in the neck of a small bottle filled with water, so that the water touches the acorn. Transfer it to a pot of soil or peat (which is the leafy soil found beneath large trees) when the roots have grown well into the water.

Try growing chestnuts and sycamore keys, planting them in a pot of peat and watering once a week.

Unroasted peanuts in their shells will grow in a pot, and they are fascinating to watch. Gently crack the middle of the peanut case to help the nuts to shoot more quickly. Put two or three in the same pot, just covering them with soil. When the shoots appear within two or three weeks, you will see their tiny clover-shaped leaves.

Try to select fruit stones from fruit which is fully ripe, as these are the most likely to grow. You can even use the stones from fruit which is beginning to decay.

Label each pot with the name of the pips or stones which have been planted, and also write the date, so that you will know how long they take to germinate.

16

ACORN

SYCAMORE   CHESTNUT

PEANUTS

Indoor Gardening
633 Hobbies and Interests, 1969.
Illustrations by B. H. Robinson.

*The Ladybird Book of
Things to Make*
633 Hobbies and Interests, 1963.
Illustrations by G. Robinson.

*The Ladybird Book of Toys and
Games to Make*
633 Hobbies and Interests, 1963.
Illustrations by Robert Ayton.

Robinson's illustrations for *Sailing and Boating*, published three years later in 1972, are more instructional in tone – gone are the happy-go-lucky children in favour of a more systematic and diagrammatic type of illustration.

John Berry's illustrations for *Learning to Ride*, first published in 1973, balance the instructional with the anatomical. The reader is guided through the bones that make up the skeleton of a horse, the parts of the body are given in meticulous detail, and the saddle and bridle deconstructed – all this just on the end-papers of the book.

Commissioning a wide range of authors and spanning a great many hobbies and interests over a period of seventeen years meant that a more extensive list of illustrators was utilized. And with a greater number of writers and artists came a greater breadth of design sensibility; the Ladybird look was certainly not static.

Sailing and Boating
633 Hobbies and Interests, 1972.
Illustrations by B. H. Robinson.

Points of sailing—reaching and running

Generally speaking, the most straightforward sailing conditions are when the wind is on the beam, that is, at right-angles to the direction of travel. In such conditions, the boom will be angled out at about forty-five degrees and the boat should move smoothly through the water. Sailing in a beam wind is known as *reaching*, and this is another point of sailing. There are two variations of the reach: one is when the wind is on the port or starboard bow, but not far enough forward to call for close-hauling. This is the *close reach*. The other variation is the *broad reach*, i.e., when the wind is from the port or starboard quarter.

The third point of sailing we are concerned with is *running* or *sailing off the wind*. This occurs when the wind is blowing from the stern area and the boat is sailing before it. In these circumstances the boom will usually be angled out as far as it will go until it is nearly at right-angles to the boat.

Running is not quite the 'plain sailing' that it appears, as we shall see. The wind direction can be critical and unless the correct line is steered relative to the wind, the boom may unexpectedly swing right across to the other side of the boat, possibly capsizing it.

16

Close Reaching

Reaching

Broad Reaching

Running

REACHING

RUNNING

Learning to Ride
633 Hobbies and Interests, 1973.
Illustrations by John Berry.

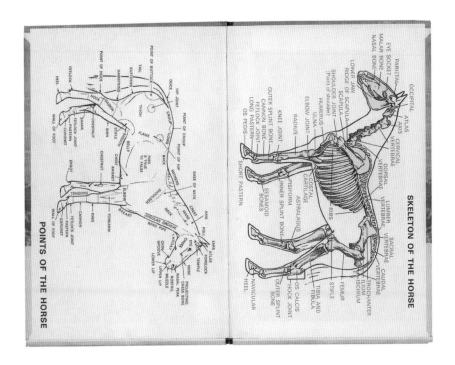

POINTS OF THE HORSE

SKELETON OF THE HORSE

Learning to Ride
633 Hobbies and Interests, 1973.
Illustrations by John Berry.

Instructional Guides

The young reader, keen to make a new toy, develop a new hobby or learn a new skill, turned to Ladybird for clear and concise guidance on all manner of topics. Swimming strokes were visually articulated from the view of the instructor, for example, and as diagrams viewed from above – giving detailed information about how to achieve the desired outcome. Detailed step-by-step instructional guides were used throughout many Ladybird titles. Ladybird's artists could be relied upon to provide the visual guidance required to learn anything from sewing to building a transistor radio or taking up fishing.

Putting on a bridle

Check that none of the bridle straps is twisted. The throat lash and the noseband must be unfastened.

Put the reins round the pony's neck and take off his halter. Hold the headpiece of the bridle in your right hand. Lay the bit on the palm of your left hand. Do not bang the bit against the pony's teeth to make him open his mouth. Tuck your fingers into the corners of his lips where he has no teeth and push his jaws apart. As you lift the bit into his mouth, pull the rest of the bridle up towards the top of his head. Gently draw his ears and forelock under the headpiece.

Fasten the throat lash so that four fingers can be placed between the strap and his cheek. Fasten the noseband so that two fingers can be slipped between the strap and his nose. The noseband itself should lie two fingers below the cheekbone. Check that the bit is just wrinkling the corners of his mouth. It is important to see that your pony is comfortable in his bridle. If anything is too tight or too loose, or the straps are not fastened down neatly, it will worry him and he will not give his full attention to his work.

See endpaper for details of a snaffle bridle.

18

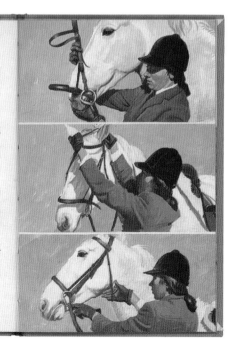

How to Swim and Dive
633 Hobbies and Interests, 1971.
Illustrations by Martin Aitchison.

Learning to Dive

Diving is actually a sport in itself and a highly specialised one. However, we are more concerned here with diving simply as a means of entering the water or to enable you to start swimming.

Your first attempts can be made standing in the water at the shallow end of the bath. Raise both hands above your head and bend forward a little from the waist (1). Bend your knees (2) and leap upward (3), at the same time bending your body (4) at the hips and tucking your head well down (5). Practise this until you can stand vertically with your hands on the bottom (6).

Next, try a sitting dive from the side of the bath. Put your feet on the side rail or trough, stretch your arms out in front of you, fingers pointing toward the water (7). Look at the bottom of the bath and topple forward into the water, pushing off with your feet as you go (8). Try to enter the water at an angle of about forty-five degrees, keeping your arms and fingers outstretched in front of your head and your body and legs in a straight line. Your feet should be together and your toes pointed backward (9).

42

Tricks and Magic

Tricks and Magic
634 Learnabout, 1969.
Illustrations by Robert Ayton.

Perhaps one of Ladybird's most popular non-fiction titles was *Tricks and Magic*. During the 1970s, magic was a big part of popular culture and Ladybird's title reflected this public interest. Studying tricks, learning the skills required to perform them and presenting them to the rest of the family was a key aspect of growing up for many boys and girls. Ladybird presented the tricks in an accessible way, with informative step-by-step visuals, yet kept the essence of mystery and intrigue so important to the young magician.

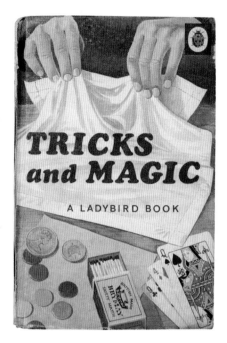

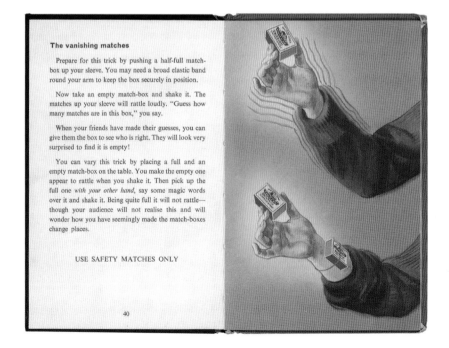

The vanishing matches

Prepare for this trick by pushing a half-full match-box up your sleeve. You may need a broad elastic band round your arm to keep the box securely in position.

Now take an empty match-box and shake it. The matches up your sleeve will rattle loudly. "Guess how many matches are in this box," you say.

When your friends have made their guesses, you can give them the box to see who is right. They will look very surprised to find it is empty!

You can vary this trick by placing a full and an empty match-box on the table. You make the empty one appear to rattle when you shake it. Then pick up the full one *with your other hand*, say some magic words over it and shake it. Being quite full it will not rattle— though your audience will not realise this and will wonder how you have seemingly made the match-boxes change places.

USE SAFETY MATCHES ONLY

40

Tricks and Magic
634 Learnabout, 1969.
Original artwork by
Robert Ayton.

A Ladybird Book about Knitting
633 Hobbies and Interests, 1972.
Illustrations by Eric Winter.

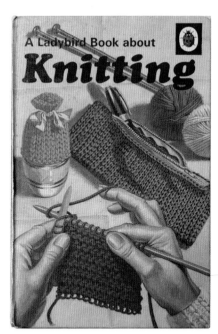

Making the purl stitch

You have learned how to make the plain stitch, so now you can learn how to make the purl stitch.

Cast on loops in the same way as you did before (page 10). Then make one row of plain stitches. When you have done this, change the needles into opposite hands so that the one which had all the stitches on is in your left hand and the empty one is in your right hand. Now you are ready to make PURL STITCHES.

Put the empty needle through the first stitch on the left-hand needle BUT this time do it from behind (Picture 1).

Wind the wool round the needle in your right hand to make a loop (Picture 2).

Pull this loop through the stitch on the left-hand needle (Picture 3).

Now leave this new stitch on the needle in your right hand while you slip off the loop from the left-hand needle (Picture 4). When you have done this, you will have made your first purl stitch.

Now you must do the same for all the other stitches on the left-hand needle. You will then have made a row of purl knitting.

22

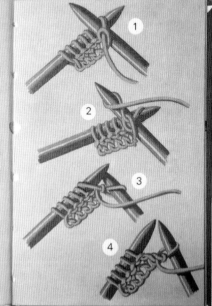

Learning to Sew
633 Hobbies and Interests, 1972.
Illustrations by Eric Winter.

Heraldry
634 Learnabout, 1974.
Illustrations by
B. H. Robinson.

Knots
634 Learnabout, 1977.
Illustrations by Eric Winter and
Frank Humphris, photography by
John Moyes and Tim Clark.

 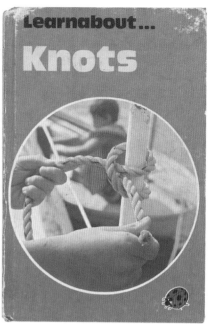

Heraldry
634 Learnabout, 1974.
Illustrations by
B. H. Robinson.

A coat-of-arms

From the illustration opposite, it is easy to imagine how a coat-of-arms may have originated.

Today, coats-of-arms are found in all sorts of places —castles, churches, town halls, on public transport, in building societies, banks, offices and schools. Some of these are not true heraldic coats-of-arms, but merely elaborate badges. Genuine lawful arms are granted by the authority of the officers of the College of Arms and are generally designed by them.

The building-up of a coat-of-arms is quite difficult, as it must be an accurate pictorial record of what is represented. Sometimes details may have to be traced back for hundreds of years.

Special technical terms are used to describe the different features. Heraldry has its own language, built up mainly from Norman-French, Latin and early English. Because heraldry first came to us from France through Germany, some of its terms are also ancient German, so it is truly a mixture of languages.

The background of a coat-of-arms is a shield (*escutcheon*), which may be one of various shapes. If the owner is an unmarried lady or a widow, it is diamond-shaped and called a *lozenge*.

The surface of this shield or lozenge is termed the *field*.

22

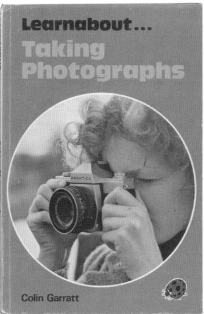

Crochet
634 Learnabout, 1975.
Illustrations by Eric Winter.

Taking Photographs
634 Learnabout, 1980.
Photography by Colin Garratt.

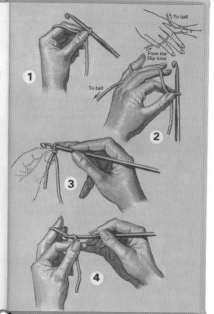

Crochet
634 Learnabout, 1975.
Illustrations by Eric Winter.

How to hold your work

1. The slip knot is now safely on the crochet hook. In the LEFT hand (or RIGHT if you are left-handed) hold the slip loop *knot* just underneath the hook, between your thumb and first finger (Picture 1).

2. From the slip loop, take the wool that leads to the ball over the first two fingers of the same hand, then under the third finger, and then right round the little finger (Picture 2).

3. Now hold the crochet hook in your RIGHT hand (or LEFT if you are left-handed), holding the crochet hook between your thumb and first finger at the flattened part of the stem. Rest your second finger on the hook, just in front of your first. Make sure the hooked end is always facing you and pointing slightly downwards (Picture 3).

4. Raise your second finger a little with the wool still going over it, so that the hooked end will be able to catch up the wool that is between your first and second fingers. Both hands, hook and wool are shown in working position in Picture 4.

You are now ready to make your first chain stitches, called *the foundation chain*, from which most crochet work grows.

10

How it Works

The popular How it Works books (series 654) spanned the years from 1965 to 1972; the first book was *The Motor Car* and the final one *The Telephone*. This series explained in simple language how fourteen different mechanical, electronic and digital modes of transport, forms of communication and industrial processes worked.

Each book in the series aimed to impart a general, but not basic, level of understanding about an aspect of modern technology. They often started from the historical perspective before explaining the scientific, technological or mechanical principles involved in making the telephone, rocket, camera, ocean liner or computer work. Whilst not a new concept, these books mixed plain speaking with informative graphics and approachable technical illustrations, often within the same piece of artwork and on the same page, to great effect.

Of the fourteen books in the series, twelve were written by David Carey, believed to be the pen name for E. C. Borst-Smith, who was assistant publicity manager at Rover Cars during the 1950s and probably linked to the company through Wills & Hepworth's commercial printing projects for Rover. Gifted at understanding and explaining how things worked, Carey authored other Ladybird titles too, including *The Ladybird Book of Motor Cars* and *A Ladybird Book of Flags*, both from Recognition (series 584).

The How it Works series also gained admiration from an older audience. *The Motor Car*, first published in 1965, was used as a general guide for car mechanics by the Thames Valley Police Driving School. University lecturers are known to have recommended *The Computer* to students at the dawn of the digital age, thus ensuring all students would start courses with the same level of knowledge. Legend has it that 200 copies of the same book were also ordered by the Ministry of Defence, but with plain covers to avoid any potential embarrassment for their staff.

Just as the People at Work series had done for Britain's industry, the How it Works series captured technology and transportation at a moment of great flux – much would change in the coming decades with the onslaught of the digital age, which was only alluded to in *The Computer*. For generations of young readers, this series did much to make sense of the technologies of a changing world.

The Motor Car
654 How it Works, 1965.
Illustrations by David Carey.

Rear Axle
Steering Wheel
Windscreen Wipers
Air Filter
Rear Lights
Filler Cap
Distributor
Engine
Plug
Carburettor
Coil
Fan
Battery
Radiator
Petrol Tank
Rear Spring
Handbrake
Propeller Shaft
Gear Stick Lever
Gearbox
Headlight
Dynamo
Drum Brake
Clutch Pedal
Brake Pedal
Accelerator Pedal
Side Light and Indicator Light
Shock Absorber
Universal Joint
Starter Motor
Steering Box
Front Suspension
Drum Brake

The Computer
654 How it Works, 1971.
Illustrations by
B. H. Robinson.

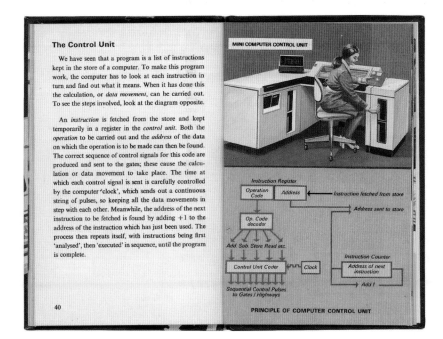

MINI COMPUTER CONTROL UNIT

The Control Unit

We have seen that a program is a list of instructions kept in the store of a computer. To make this program work, the computer has to look at each instruction in turn and find out what it means. When it has done this the calculation, or *data movement*, can be carried out. To see the steps involved, look at the diagram opposite.

An *instruction* is fetched from the store and kept temporarily in a register in the *control unit*. Both the *operation* to be carried out and the *address* of the data on which the operation is to be made can then be found. The correct sequence of control signals for this code are produced and sent to the gates; these cause the calculation or data movement to take place. The time at which each control signal is sent is carefully controlled by the computer 'clock', which sends out a continuous string of pulses, so keeping all the data movements in step with each other. Meanwhile, the address of the next instruction to be fetched is found by adding +1 to the address of the instruction which has just been used. The process then repeats itself, with instructions being first 'analysed', then 'executed' in sequence, until the program is complete.

40

Instruction Register
Operation Code
Address
Instruction fetched from store
Address sent to store
Op. Code decoder
Add. Sub. Store Read etc.
Instruction Counter
Address of next instruction
Control Unit Coder
Clock
Add 1
Sequential Control Pulses to Gates / Highways

PRINCIPLE OF COMPUTER CONTROL UNIT

Television
654 How it Works, 1968.
Illustrations by B. H. Robinson.

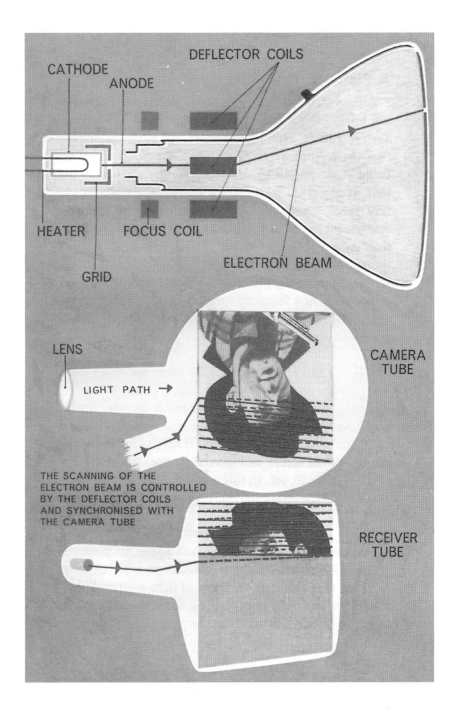

CATHODE
ANODE
DEFLECTOR COILS
HEATER
FOCUS COIL
GRID
ELECTRON BEAM

LENS
LIGHT PATH →
CAMERA TUBE

THE SCANNING OF THE
ELECTRON BEAM IS CONTROLLED
BY THE DEFLECTOR COILS
AND SYNCHRONISED WITH
THE CAMERA TUBE

RECEIVER TUBE

Ladybird by Design

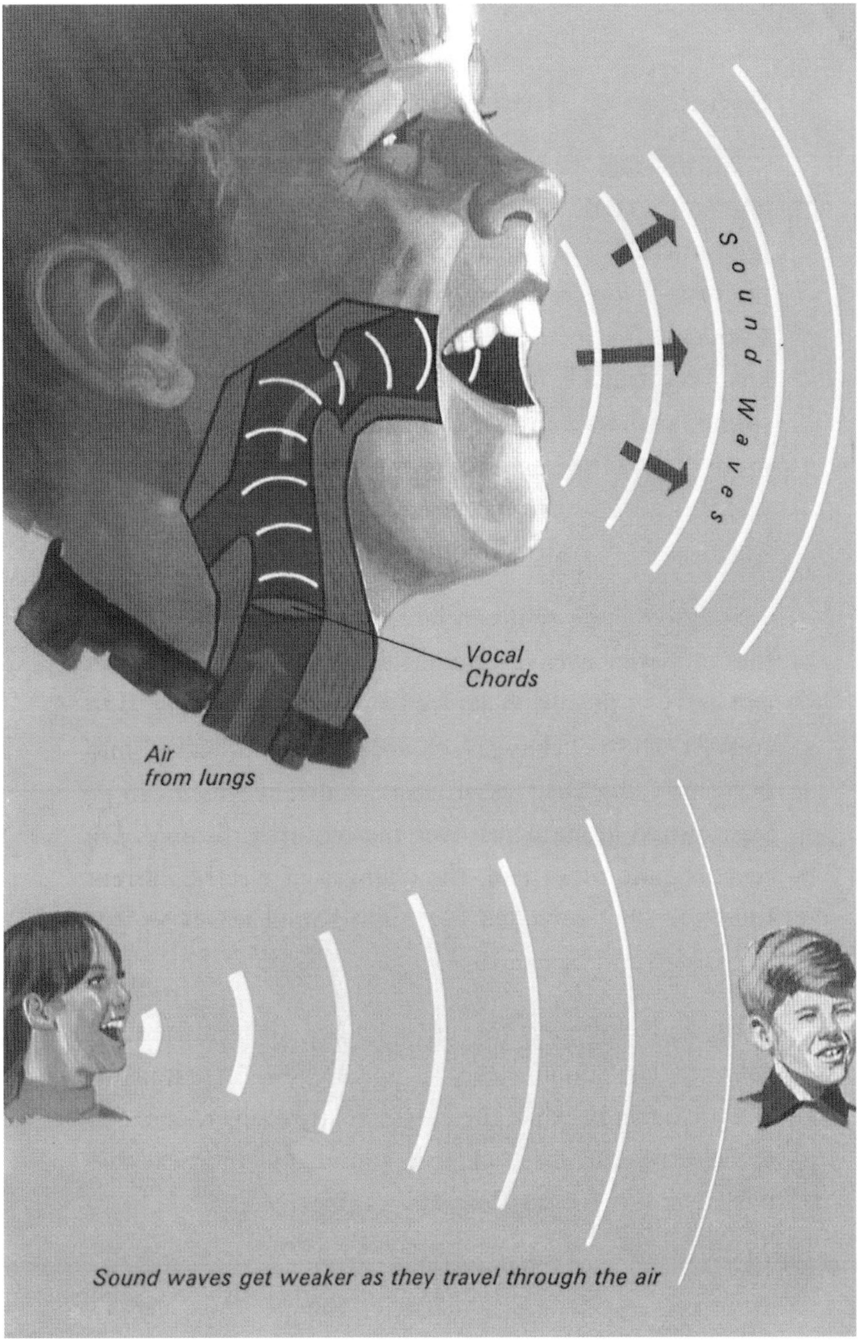

The Telephone
654 How it Works, 1972.
Illustrations by B. H. Robinson.

Sound Waves

Vocal
Chords

Air
from lungs

Sound waves get weaker as they travel through the air

The Electron Gun

The electrical charges in the caesium dots cannot be released without help. The next step is to get each tiny charge to set up electrical *currents* which can be amplified (made stronger) and transmitted as *electro-magnetic radio waves* to our television aerials.

This is done by the *electron gun*. It is a device which shoots out a stream of electrons in the form of a needle-like beam, rather like a machine-gun shooting out bullets, only much faster. Magnetic deflector coils, or plates, are placed around the muzzle of the gun and, by adjusting the electrical current flowing through them, the gun can be aimed in such a way that its beam sweeps back and forth, and also up and down, across the mosaic screen. The movement of the electron beam is the same as that of your eyes when you read this book—from left to right. This sweeping action is known as *scanning*.

The electron beam scans the whole mosaic screen fifty times every second, releasing the various electrical charges from all the caesium dots as it passes over them. These charges of current are then sent through an amplifier to make them stronger, and eventually transformed into electro-magnetic radio waves which radiate from the transmitting aerial. Just as the electrical charges in the dots are large or small according to the amount of light that has fallen on them, so the electron beam produces a large or small change of electrical current as it scans the dots.

12

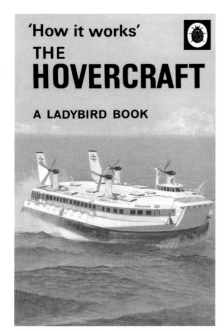

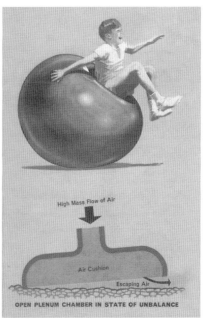

OPEN PLENUM CHAMBER IN STATE OF UNBALANCE

The Hovercraft
654 How it Works, 1969.
Illustrations by B. H. Robinson.

Skirts

Workable hovercraft can be built using a plenum chamber employing the momentum curtain technique. In fact, the first one to cross the English Channel used this system. However, the hover height was still too low unless great, and uneconomical, power was used. Simple obstacles such as quite small waves, or a tide-formed ridge of shingle on a beach, could prove inconvenient.

These problems led to the development of the 'skirt'. This is a shaped, flexible skirt fitted below the bottom edges of the plenum chamber slot. As the hovercraft lifts, the skirt extends below it to retain a much deeper cushion of air. The development of the skirt enables a hovercraft to maintain its normal operating speed through quite large waves. It also enables it to pass over boulders or ridges.

The skirt of a hovercraft is one of its most sensitive parts. The design must be just right, or an uncomfortable ride results. Also, excessive wear of the skirt can occur if its edges are flapping up and down on the surface of the sea.

12

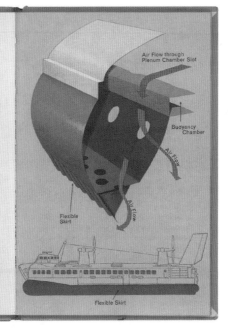

II. A Design for Life

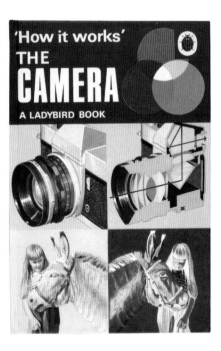

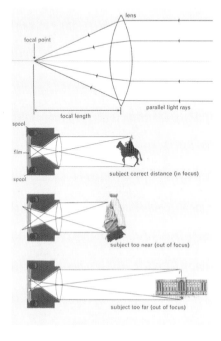

B. H. Robinson

The illustrator of the How it Works series, Bernard Herbert Robinson, was born in 1930 and trained at Croydon Art School. Robinson was an accomplished illustrator with a distinctive style and approach, working with pencil and water-colour paints on art-board. His compositions were perfectly considered, intuitively balancing images of contemporary scenes with infographics; in *The Telephone* infographics expertly illustrate the concept of sound waves. His stylistic approach perfectly explained the modern world and its many complexities to a young audience.

Working for Ladybird from 1965 to 1980, Robinson created images for numerous series, including Achievements (series 601) and Learnabout (series 634). Whilst tackling diverse subject matter, his work was easily recognizable. His approach was more free than the Ladybird illustrators before him, and his images seemed to be more in tune with a 1970s aesthetic – children wore their hair longer, just as he did, and the style was looser and more contemporary. Robinson continued illustrating until around 2000 and died in 2004 aged seventy-four.

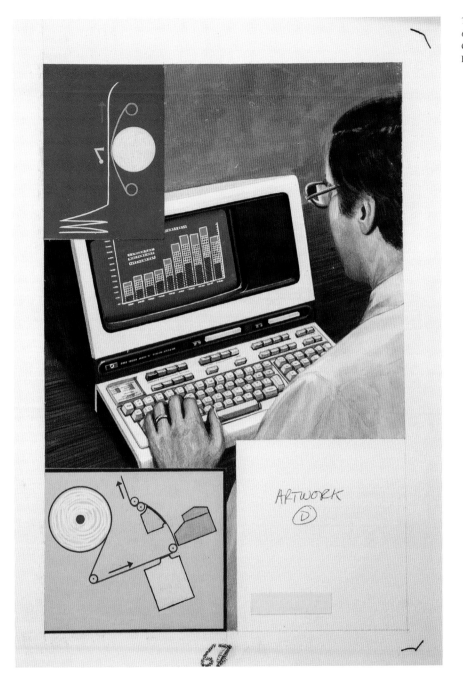

Typographic Treatments

For the most part, the best aspects of Ladybird's design aesthetic were evident in the work of the numerous illustrators and commercial artists – there was always a level of craftsmanship and attention to detail that ensured Ladybird books stood out from their competitors.

However, Ladybird also utilized font design to give greater resonance to the covers of certain titles, as seen in the designs for *The Computer* and *The Telephone* (series 654), the digital-looking font in keeping with the graphic style of the time. The world was waking up to techno-logical and digital advances and this choice of font represents how this was perceived at the time.

Ladybird's designers, for the most part, reflected a changing world around them; whilst perhaps not at the cutting edge of contemporary graphic design, their covers were designed with sincerity and an understanding of their audience of children, parents and teachers.

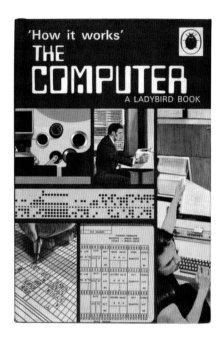

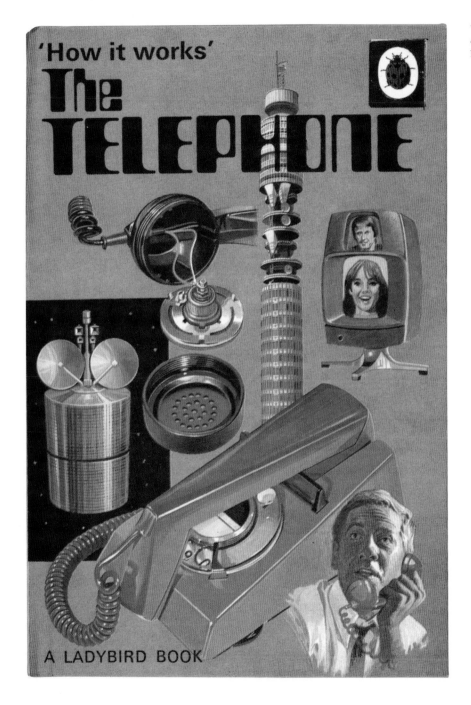

'How it works'
The TELEPHONE
A LADYBIRD BOOK

The Telephone
654 How it Works, 1972.
Illustrations by B. H. Robinson.

III. Key Words and Key Images

Ladybird's voice was that of a friendly teacher, an older guiding brother or sister, a knowledgeable uncle or aunt: never patronizing, always optimistic and forever British.

Ladybird's Artists

In today's media-saturated world it is hard to imagine a time before the photographic image held such a prominent position in society, when the go-to image-maker for book jackets, advertising campaigns and posters was the graphic artist. The photographic image would come to prominence across most fields of communication, but the children's book would be the final bastion of illustration by enthralling generations of young readers, tapping into and feeding their imaginations in ways that only illustration can.

Illustration has often been referred to as 'the people's art'; understood and enjoyed by all, and designed to speak to us and reflect the lives we lead. For many, Ladybird books may have been the first introduction to the medium of illustration, a connection that continued from children's books and comics to school text books, and on to adult fiction book covers, record and CD sleeves, and magazine articles.

Ladybird's reliance on illustration and the work of master illustrators cannot be overestimated. Whilst the stories of the Well-loved Tales were beautifully written, the research behind the Key Words Reading Scheme thorough and well-articulated, and the scientific knowledge in the Junior Science series informative and educational, it was the work of many of Britain's most talented graphic artists and illustrators that brought the books to life.

After the Second World War, Ladybird was to become the by-word for quality in children's book publishing. The calibre and quality of the work of

PREVIOUS PAGE:
3a Things We Like
641 Key Words, 1964.
Original artwork by
Martin Aitchison.

3a Things We Like
641 Key Words, 1964.
Illustrations by
Martin Aitchison.

Ladybird's small army of illustrators was remarkable, and many artists viewed working for Ladybird Books as the pinnacle of their careers. Most artists worked on a freelance basis, creating twenty-four illustrations for one title, and possibly many more if they were asked to work on numerous books within a series. For the jobbing artist, a Ladybird commission would mean an intensive but well-paid job, and certainly a welcome dividend in post-war Britain, when generating an income as a freelancer would have been uncertain.

Ladybird provided gainful employment for numerous illustrators and in return requested reliability. Artists were expected to meet deadlines as production schedules could not be held up waiting for artwork to arrive. It was also vital for a set of twenty-four illustrations to retain a consistent visual aesthetic. Added to this, Ladybird expected a positive work ethic and illustrators were often introduced to writers so they could work together to bring stories and themes to life. This is believed to have helped with the relationship between text and image that was critical to the success of Ladybird titles. Of course, it was a given that the Ladybird illustrator would be an accomplished artist. Stunning craftsmanship, with attention to detail, was simply an expectation for those illustrators commissioned to work with the publishers.

FROM TOP LEFT TO BOTTOM RIGHT:
B. H. Robinson.
Illustrator of many books in the Achievements (601) and How it Works (654) series.

Charles Tunnicliffe.
Illustrator of classic Ladybird natural history titles including the *What to Look For* books (series 536), shown making an engraving in his studio.

Robert Ayton.
He illustrated many of Ladybird's 'Golden Age' titles such as books in the Achievements (601) and Hobbies (633) series.

John Kenney.
Illustrator of *Tootles the Taxi* (series 413) and many of the titles in the Adventures from History series (561).

Frank Hampson.
Illustrator of the two *Kings and Queens* books (series 561), as well as titles from Fairy Tales and Rhymes (series 413).

Martin Aitchison.
He worked for Ladybird for almost thirty years, illustrating books for series as diverse as Key Words (series 641), Lives of the Great Composers (series 662) and Puddle Lane (series 855).

J. H. Wingfield.
Known as Harry, he famously illustrated many of the most popular Ladybird books, including Key Words (series 641), Well-loved Tales (series 606D) and Learning with Mother (series 702).

Frank Humphris.
An artist with a passion for the American West, he wrote and illustrated three titles in General Interest (series 707), including *The Story of the Cowboy*, and created art for some of the later titles in the Adventures from History series (561).

Ladybird Logos

Most companies that have been in existence over many decades refine and update their logos over time and Ladybird has proved no exception. As well as gracing the front of the books, the Ladybird logo has appeared in many different guises. It was printed as a repeat pattern in light brown on the end-papers of books between 1953 and 1960, and then in light blue between 1956 and 1961, when the first redesign of the Ladybird logo was unveiled.

1915

1915

The first Ladybird logo, in use from 1915, depicted a ladybird with outstretched wings. With hand-rendered typography and showing a ladybird in flight, it was reproduced in single colours – printed in either black, pale blue or green. Despite, or perhaps because of, its quirky nature, the original logo remained in use and unchanged for another four decades.

1961

The revised Ladybird logo had a more contemporary feel and stronger graphic edge. It was based on a real ladybird chosen by Douglas Keen from specimens at the National History Museum and was reproduced in black line with a keyline lozenge holding the ladybird in position.

1965

Just four years later, the logo was updated, with the distinctive red body of the ladybird placed on a white lozenge within a black box.

1966

The following year saw the introduction of a new logo specifically created for the Key Words Reading Scheme. It incorporated the new Ladybird logo into an image of a key – an obvious graphic choice which nonetheless created a striking image.

Ladybird by Design

Whilst the evolution of Ladybird's logo reflected the publishing company's growth and the popularity of the books, the logos can't be considered examples of truly inspirational graphic design. The logos performed their roles well: they were understated and unassuming yet also retained an air of confidence. Fairly traditional in design terms, a Ladybird logo was the mark of a great product, whilst never being an innovative mark in itself.

2015

1967

A more three-dimensional ladybird then appeared. Existing without the visual constraints of a box or border, the new ladybird appeared to be crawling across the page or cover of the books.

1993

In the early 1990s the Ladybird name was reintroduced to the logo, this time with a ladybird crawling along the upper edge of the box in which the logo sat. The dot of the 'i' forms one of the ladybird's spots.

2006

This is the most recent redesign. A redrawn, more cartoon-like ladybird character, it takes its visual cues from the 1961 Ladybird logo. Viewed from above, once again, and placed in its own distinctive ellipse, today's logo retains and recalls a sense of its heritage, whilst reflecting Ladybird's status as a modern, forward-facing children's publisher.

Ladybird Typography

The design of Ladybird's typography was an integral aspect of the Ladybird reading experience. The layout and application of its fonts and typefaces was critical to the reader's understanding and enjoyment of the book, whether he or she was being read to, learning to read or was a more confident, independent reader. In the early post-war years, it is likely that design decisions were made by printing staff at Wills & Hepworth, as was common at the time. Later, in-house designers would have taken over much of the decision-making.

Typography in children's book publishing was no doubt influenced by research conducted at the end of the 19th century by medical practitioners and psychologists who explored the effect of reading and writing on eyesight. This led to the recommendations that type size should be large and well-proportioned, and that line lengths be kept to a minimum. By the early 20th century, the British Association of Science had published sample tables specifying ideal type sizes for children of differing ages – ostensibly suggesting that the younger the child, the larger the type.

Another key contributing factor that would influence the page design of Ladybird books was, of course, the available technology. By the 1930s, printing journals were beginning to show an interest in children's book production, making further recommendations for the use of typography. Monotype, the mechanized type-composing system used universally by publishers, responded by promoting newly cut typefaces with accompanying type specimens, showing typefaces in situ with the most appropriate leading and spacing. In effect, they provided sample layouts, advising that for children's books there should be ample space between words and lines.

Ladybird would vary its typographic design decisions from book to book, depending on its audience – and whilst there might be consistency within a series, changes occurred from series to series as different design and typographic approaches, and most probably new staff, came into the production process.

Ladybird also introduced handwritten typefaces to some of the books aimed at early readers, likely in response to a view first formed by school teachers in the 1920s that children learned to read more swiftly from handwritten rather than printed script. Ladybird was still using handwritten

Example of a monotype machine.

The Story of Printing
601 Achievements, 1970.
Illustrations by Robert Ayton.

launched the Key Words Reading Scheme in 1964, although for consistency it had most likely been developed into a stencil as there were no visible differences between the typefaces. With the introduction of computer software in the 1990s, the handwritten typeface was developed into a digital typeface allowing much more control and greater ease of application.

In keeping with Ladybird's view that the Key Words Reading Scheme would improve reading skills level by level, a total of four different typefaces were used across the scheme. The handwritten type was used for all the books in levels 1 and 2. For levels 3, 4, 5 and 6, Gill Sans, a sans-serif font designed by Eric Gill and first released by Monotype in 1928, was used for clear legibility. As the young reader grew in confidence, the line lengths grew and the type size scaled down – for levels 7, 8 and 9 Ladybird chose a slab serif font close in style to the Century Schoolbook font, designed by Morris Fuller Benton in 1919 for the American Type Founders (ATF). The final levels 10, 11 and 12 used Times New Roman, another serif font, first commissioned by *The Times* newspaper in 1931 and designed by Victor Lardent for Monotype.

In many of the Key Words books, the text was justified, meaning each line of text was exactly the same length, a stylistic practice that led to differing spaces between words. In all other aspects, the choice of typeface and its arrangement on the page was attuned perfectly for the early reader, following the extensive research by William Murray, the creator of the Key Words Reading Scheme, into how best to lay out the text for Ladybird's young audience. The easy letter shapes of the handwritten sans-serif font were suited to those beginning to read, whilst more confident readers could practise reading the different letter shapes of the serif fonts featured in the later Key Words books.

An example of the hand-lettered Ladybird font.

Telling the Time
563 Learning to Read, 1962.
Illustrations by J. H. Wingfield.

An example of the hand-lettered Ladybird font.

Helping at Home
563 Learning to Read, 1961.
Illustrations by J. H. Wingfield.

An example of the simple, handwritten Ladybird typeface used in levels 1 and 2.

2c I Like to Write
641 Key Words, 1965.
Illustrations by
Martin Aitchison.

An example of the sans-serif Gill Sans font used in levels 3, 4, 5 and 6.

5c More Sounds to Say
641 Key Words, 1965.
Illustrations by
J. H. Wingfield.

28

Yes   No

1 Is Jane here ? ──.
2 Is Peter here ? ───.
3 Is the dog here ? ──.
4 Has Peter a fish? ──.

The answers are on Page 49

12 Here is an orange.
O   Say the word orange.
    What is the sound
      when you start to say **orange** ?   O

    Here is an ostrich.
O   Say the word ostrich.
    You make the **o** sound
      when you start to say **ostrich** .   O

    Here is an ox.
O   Say the word ox.
    What is the sound
      when you start to say **ox** ?   O

    Here is an otter.
O   Say the word otter.
    You make the **o** sound
      when you start to say **otter** .   O

Ladybird by Design

12

Father and Peter have to wait some time for Mother and Jane. Then Peter says, "I can see them now. Here they are."

Mother has bought a new hat. "I hope you like the hat I have bought," she says.

"I like it," says Peter. "You have found a nice one."

"Yes, you have picked a nice one," says Father. "I think it is lovely. We both like it."

Mother looks happy. "A woman always likes a new hat," she says. "I have not bought another hat this year."

"We had to wait a long time," Peter says to Jane. "It made me think you were lost."

"When are we going to see the big garden?" asks Jane. "Can we go today?"

Father says, "We have too much to do today. We will go over in two days' time. I put that in my letter to Mr White. I want to see him before he goes away. We should have a talk before he goes. Come on now, it is five o'clock and time to go home."

An example of the slab serif font used in levels 7, 8 and 9.

8b The Big House
641 Key Words, 1966.
Illustrations by
Martin Aitchison.

38

The two children and their uncle entered the helicopter. Uncle showed them the safety straps on each seat. "We must fasten these safety straps," he said. "Please put them on now."

As they fastened the safety straps, Uncle explained how useful they were in times of accident.

They sat back and looked out of the helicopter as Uncle made it rise in the air.

"It seems to rise quickly," said Jane to Peter. "I did not know that helicopters could go so fast." "We can see a long way," Peter said. "Is that the island in the distance?" he asked. His uncle answered that it was, and said that he would fly the helicopter that way.

Soon they were flying over the island. "This is useful," said Peter, looking down. "We may be able to see the boy."

Uncle made the helicopter fly low down so that it was near the tops of the trees. Suddenly they saw the boy. He was in the woods looking up at them. Then he disappeared.

"He must have jumped into that hollow tree again," said Peter. He explained to his uncle how the boy had hidden in a hollow tree during the search for him the day before.

An example of the Times New Roman font used in levels 10, 11 and 12.

11a Mystery on the Island
641 Key Words, 1966.
Illustrations by
Martin Aitchison.

Ladybird Language

Ladybird's editorial style and approach was, in many ways, unique. With its vast array of subject areas spanning fiction and non-fiction, no other children's book publisher covered as much ground with such apparent ease. The Ladybird tone of voice and language was an essential component to each title.

Well-researched, well-edited, accurate, honest and trusted, the Ladybird language was informative without being prescriptive, distinctive without being revolutionary and straightforward without ever being dull. It spoke with confidence, yet with a simple no-nonsense editorial style. Ladybird's voice was that of a friendly teacher, an older guiding brother or sister, a knowledgeable uncle or aunt: never patronizing, always optimistic and forever British.

At a time when the British Empire had yet to decline and the combined colonies still represented one-fifth of the world's population, Ladybird's overtly British view of the world was one that reflected a nation growing in confidence and prosperity following the end of the Second World War. If a Ladybird book were to have had a voice, it would most likely have sounded like a radio or TV presenter from the 1950s or 1960s, with every syllable articulated precisely, every expression nuanced perfectly and every sentence grammatically impeccable.

Ladybird books were consistently researched, with Douglas Keen commissioning expert storytellers, historians, scientists and educators. Two of the country's most eminent educationalists, William Murray, a head teacher, and Joe McNally, an educational psychologist, were asked to turn their research into a series of books that became the Key Words Reading Scheme (series 641). Vera Southgate, an educationalist employed by the University of Manchester between 1960 and 1979, was commissioned to retell popular fairy tales for the Well-loved Tales (series 606D).

Other notable writers included Lawrence du Garde Peach, who penned the successful Adventures from History books (series 561), which comprised over thirty titles. An author and playwright for radio, stage and screen, he earned a PhD for a thesis on 17th century drama and an OBE for services to literature in 1972.

ABC
455 Uncle Mac, 1950.
Illustrations by Sep. E. Scott.

Also awarded an OBE was Derek Ivor Breashur McCulloch, known as Uncle Mac, the name behind Ladybird's six educational titles in series 455. As Uncle Mac, he was a popular BBC radio announcer, producer and writer. He was the voice of Larry the Lamb, and the presenter of *Children's Hour* and the popular Saturday-morning children's request programme *Children's Favourites* between 1954 and 1965. A well-known and trusted BBC figure, Uncle Mac and Ladybird seemed like the perfect union.

Ladybird clearly understood the importance of commissioning high-profile figures to lend their names to titles, as well as some of the best experts in their field to research and write their books. As a consequence, many of Ladybird's books were exquisitely written, the language of Ladybird accessible and consistently high-quality. Its editorial approach reflected the views that the nation had of itself: proud to be British, and proud to entertain and educate children.

9c Enjoying Reading
641 Key Words, 1966.
Illustrations by
Martin Aitchison.

40

The girl comes out of the house into the garden to pick some apples. She wants to give some to a friend. There is a wasp on an apple but the girl does not see it. She puts her hand on the apple and the wasp stings her. The sting hurts the girl. She calls out and runs into the house to her mother.

The girl tells her mother about the wasp and points to the sting on her hand. Her mother puts something on it. Soon it does not hurt. Then she helps her to pick some apples for her friend.

Copy out and complete—

1. A wa-- is on an apple.
2. The wasp h--ts the girl.
3. She p--nts to the sting.
4. Mother looks at the st---.
5 They pi-- some apples.
6 The apples are f-- her friend.

The answers are on Page 49

The Musicians of Bremen
606D Well-loved Tales, 1974.
Illustrations by Robert Lumley
and John Berry.

Then the donkey gave the signal, by nodding his head, and they all began to make music together.

The donkey brayed, the dog barked, the cat miaowed and the cock crowed at the top of his voice. You never heard such a terrible noise in all your life!

30

On a glorious August morning Henry V of England landed on the shore of Normandy, which his ancestors had ruled and which he claimed as his own. There was no resistance. The French forces were gathered in the fortress of Harfleur, nearby.

The ships had been run on the beach in shallow water, but instead of leaping ashore, the soldiers remained on board, watching and waiting. Henry had given strict orders that no-one was to land until he himself was on shore. In full armour he strode through the shallow waves and fell on his knees, praying for victory over his enemies. As he did so, the King's Choristers aboard the *Trinité Royale* sang a psalm.

The King rose from his knees and the soldiers swarmed ashore. It was a busy scene as thousands of men and horses were landed. Everywhere the men were struggling with the heavy weapons and the many stores needed for an army of 30,000 men.

By nightfall all had landed, and Henry could discuss the next move with his knights.

32

The Story of Henry V 561 Adventures from History, 1962. Illustrations by John Kenney.

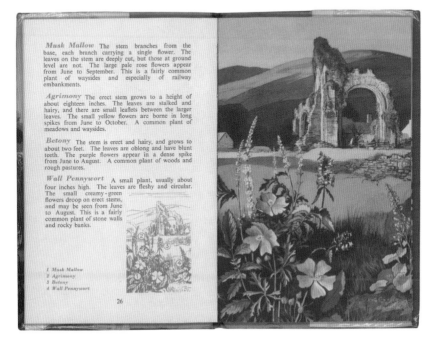

Musk Mallow The stem branches from the base, each branch carrying a single flower. The leaves on the stem are deeply cut, but those at ground level are not. The large pale rose flowers appear from June to September. This is a fairly common plant of waysides and especially of railway embankments.

Agrimony The erect stem grows to a height of about eighteen inches. The leaves are stalked and hairy, and there are small leaflets between the larger leaves. The small yellow flowers are borne in long spikes from June to October. A common plant of meadows and waysides.

Betony The stem is erect and hairy, and grows to about two feet. The leaves are oblong and have blunt teeth. The purple flowers appear in a dense spike from June to August. A common plant of woods and rough pastures.

Wall Pennywort A small plant, usually about four inches high. The leaves are fleshy and circular. The small creamy-green flowers droop on erect stems, and may be seen from June to August. This is a fairly common plant of stone walls and rocky banks.

1 Musk Mallow
2 Agrimony
3 Betony
4 Wall Pennywort

26

The Ladybird Book of British Wild Flowers 536 Nature, 1957. Illustrations by Rowland and Edith Hilder.

III. Key Words and Key Images

Foreign Editions

It is estimated that Ladybird books have been published in approximately seventy different languages and dialects including Afrikaans, Arabic, Chinese, Esperanto, Icelandic, Irish Gaelic, Japanese, Malay, Swedish, Turkish, Welsh and Zulu.

Starting in the 1950s with a small number of titles being translated into French and Afrikaans, by the early 1970s Ladybird books were being exported all over the world.

In the 1970s Ladybird also began working with an Arabic publisher to translate titles into Arabic. This was challenging; firstly because the books needed to reproduced to be read from back to front with the spine on the right-hand side and, secondly, because strict cultural differences meant that artwork suitable for the British market had to be revised to comply with Middle Eastern sensibilities.

Ladybird also provided translations in Esperanto, the politically neutral language created by L. L. Zamenhof in 1887, and into ITA, the Initial Teaching Alphabet, a variant of the Latin alphabet developed by Sir James Pitman that was briefly popular in the 1960s.

Initial Teaching Alphabet (ITA) edition of *Puppies and Kittens* 563 Learning to Read, 1968. Illustrations by Harry Woolley.

Arabic edition of *Bunnikin's Picnic Party* 401 Animal Stories Told in Verse, *c.*1982. Illustrations by A. J. MacGregor.

Ladybird by Design

Esperanto edition of
The Ladybird Book of London
618 Capital Cities of the World,
1971. Illustrations by John Berry.

Serbo-Croat edition of
The Rocket
654 How it Works, 1970.
Illustrations by B. H. Robinson.

Maltese edition of
Helping at Home
563 Learning to Read, 1973.
Illustrations by J. H. Wingfield.

Irish Gaelic edition of
Snow-White and the Seven Dwarfs
606D Well-loved Tales, 1972.
Illustrations by Eric Winter.

Danish edition of
*The Lord's Prayer and
Other Prayers for Children*
612 Prayers and Hymns, 1967.
Illustrations by J. H. Wingfield.

Afrikaans edition of
Mick the Disobedient Puppy
497 Animal Stories, 1953.
Illustrations by P. B. Hickling.

German edition of
The Story of Flight
601 Achievements, 1972.
Illustrations by Robert Ayton.

Welsh edition of
1a Play With Us
641 Key Words, 1969.
Illustrations by J. H. Wingfield.

French edition of
The Three Little Pigs
606D Well-loved Tales, 1983.
Illustrations by Robert Lumley.

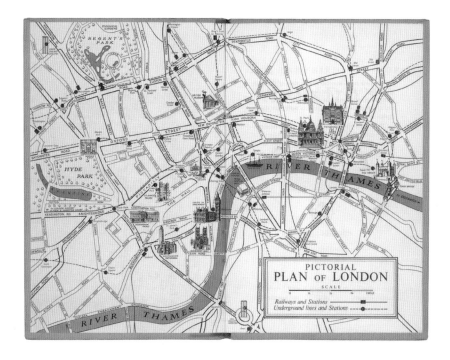

End-papers

The twenty-four illustrations in each Ladybird book were often supplemented by beautifully crafted end-papers that were additional pieces of art, technical or diagrammatic illustrations, or reproduced maps.

This added extra for the young reader was proof, if needed, that Ladybird had thought of everything – an illustrated end-paper could add further detailed knowledge to the subject as in the black-and-white natural history illustrations of the bills, feet and eggs on the end-papers of *Sea and Estuary Birds*, or provide useful geographic reference with a pictorial plan of London in the front end-paper and a redesign of Harry Beck's London Underground map by Harold F. Hutchinson at the back of *The Ladybird Book of London*.

The end-papers for *The Story of our Churches and Cathedrals* are useful illustrated guides to the layout of a typical cathedral and village church as well as to the various doorways, windows and types of arch construction to be found – a treasure trove of additional architectural detail.

Ladybird by Design

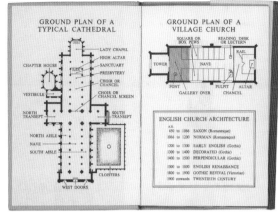

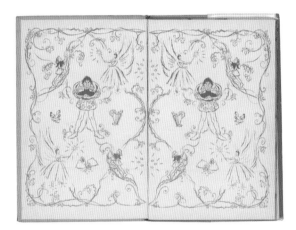

End-papers could be decorative as well as informative, and were an opportunity for the Ladybird artist to extend an illustration from within the book, as in the blue-line illustrations by A. J. MacGregor for the end-papers of *Downy Duckling*, or the mix of fairy tale characters seen at the front and back of the Well-loved Tales series.

IV. Modern-day Ladybird

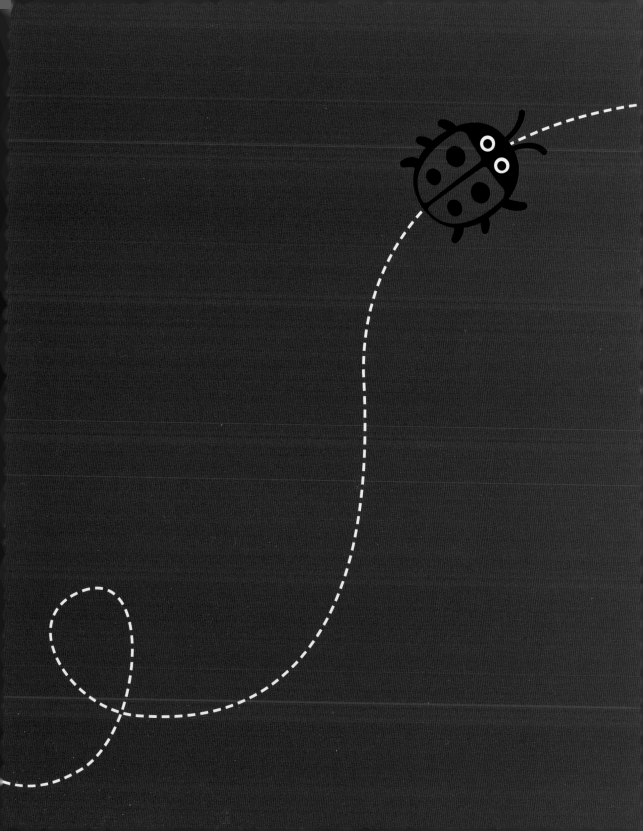

Ladybird retains both its prominent position as one of the UK's foremost children's book publishers and its almost unprecedented brand name awareness amongst consumers.

Ladybird Lifestyle

Ladybird's Loughborough offices in the 1970s.

The early 1970s saw Ladybird entering a new era of change. Firstly, the introduction of decimalization on 15 February 1971 led to a new pricing structure and the cost of Ladybird books became 12½p. That summer the company revised the price to 15p, the first permanent price increase in over thirty years. (An increase had been trialled years earlier, but with a drop in sales the price soon reverted to its original 2/6d.)

The following year, in preparation for managing director James Shields Clegg's imminent retirement, Wills & Hepworth approached the Pearson Longman Group with a view to selling the company to secure its longevity. Pearson had acquired Penguin Books in 1970 following the terminal illness of Penguin's controlling shareholder Allen Lane, and was seen as the best publishing company to ensure the future of Ladybird Books and protect the well-being of the staff.

On 3 January 1972 Wills & Hepworth and the Ladybird imprint became the property of the Pearson Longman Group for the sum of £3.37 million, approximately £41.6 millon in today's money. In September of that year, Wills & Hepworth officially changed its name to Ladybird Books.

Both the sale to the Pearson Longman Group and the move to new premises were to signal change of an unprecedented nature at the publishing company. Later in 1972, 2.25 acres of land in Loughborough were purchased and building work was completed to house all aspects of Ladybird's operations in one place – the printing presses, bindery, warehousing and offices for all Ladybird staff. In 1974, James Shields Clegg, who had joined Wills & Hepworth Ltd in 1934 and played a major part in taking Ladybird books to vast new audiences, retired from his role as managing director. Early the following year, the inspirational editorial director, Douglas Keen, also retired. Ladybird was now without two of its key personnel in place to guide future progress.

Ladybird by Design

Talkabout Baby
735 Talkabout, 1974.
Collage cover artist unknown.

Talkabout Home
735 Talkabout, 1973.
Collage cover artist unknown.

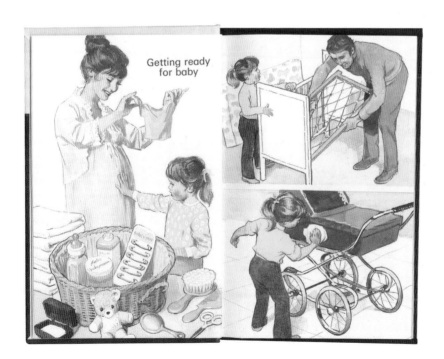

Getting ready
for baby

Talkabout Baby
735 Talkabout, 1974.
Interior illustrations by
Harry Wingfield.

Teeth
737 Leaders, 1978.
Illustrations by Vernon Mills,
Jorge Nuñez and Gerald Whitcomb.

Water
737 Leaders, 1973.
Illustrations by
Gerald Whitcomb.

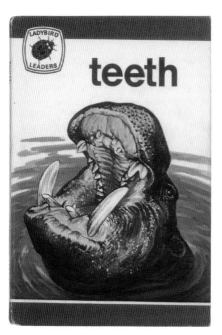

Teeth
737 Leaders, 1978.
Illustrations by Vernon Mills,
Jorge Nuñez and Gerald Whitcomb.

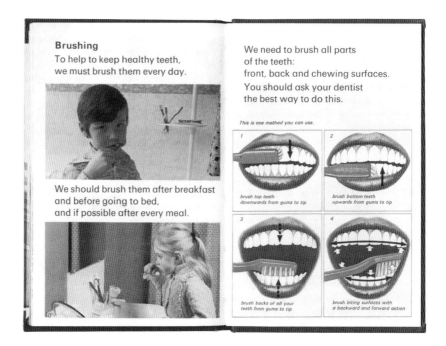

Ladybird by Design

During the 1970s, Ladybird began reissuing previous titles with new covers and many with updated illustrations, while still continuing to create many brand-new series with different looks.

The Talkabout books (series 735) were aimed at parents with toddlers. These titles made a radical departure from the design of Ladybird's classic years – whilst keeping the classic format, they featured collaged illustrations on the covers. They still appealed to young children but demonstrated a dramatic move away from the Ladybird books of old.

Ladybird Leaders (series 737) followed. Primarily aimed at reluctant readers and older children, the titles covered a vast array of non-fiction subjects, such as *Deserts*, *Air*, *Under the Ground*, *Seals and Whales*, *Coffee*, *Fire*, *Bread* and *Polar Regions*. There may have appeared little rhyme or reason to the grouping of the topics in the series, but the subject matter and vocabulary across all titles was chosen specifically by experts and the simple text was displayed in large sans-serif typography to ensure ease of reading. In this sense, Ladybird's working methods remained largely unchanged.

Series 740 retold famous tales such as *Aesop's Fables*, *Treasure Island*, *The Swiss Family Robinson* and *A Journey to the Centre of the Earth* in simpler language and with colourful pictures, making them accessible for younger readers.

Ali Baba and the Forty Thieves
740 Fables and Legends, 1975.
Illustrations by Robert Ayton.

Famous Legends Book 1
740 Fables and Legends, 1975.
Illustrations by Robert Ayton.

Cinderella
777 Read it Yourself, 1978.
Illustrations by
Brian Price Thomas.

Goldilocks & the 3 Bears
777 Read it Yourself, 1977.
Illustrations by John Dyke.

Cinderella
777 Read it Yourself, 1978.
Illustrations by
Brian Price Thomas.

Ladybird by Design

Penelope Strawberry and Roger Radish
793 The Garden Gang, 1979.
Illustrations by Jayne Fisher.

Avril Apricot and Simon Swede
793 The Garden Gang, 1980.
Illustrations by Jayne Fisher.

Read it Yourself (series 777) consisted of twenty-four titles aimed at young children who had grasped the basics of reading. Each title retold a classic fairy tale and had a bold and distinctive cover, with the large series title printed in a bright contemporary colour inside a black panel. Ladybird was making unconventional and bold moves forward in the design of their new titles – and nowhere more so than in 1979 when they took the rather unusual step of publishing a range of books written and illustrated by a child.

The Garden Gang (series 793) was a set of stories created about characters based on fruit and vegetables. At just nine years old, Jayne Fisher was to become Ladybird's youngest author and artist – with seventeen titles in the series in total, including an annual and two colouring books, this was no small feat. Jayne created all twenty-four illustrations for each of the storybooks, hand-drawing them with felt-tipped pens in bright primary colours. There is something very endearing about Fisher's characters – her quirky, simple drawings exude personality.

Wee Willie Water Melon and Betty Beetroot, Gertrude Gooseberry and Belinda Blackcurrant, Penelope Strawberry and Roger Radish looked child-like yet delightfully expressive, and they came to life in her engaging and optimistic stories.

How to Make Wooden Toys
633 Hobbies and Interests, 1979.
Photography by John Moyes.

How to Make Dolls
633 Hobbies and Interests, 1978.
Photography by John Moyes.

The Fire Service
822 People Who Help Us, 1982.
Photography by Tim Clark.

The Police Force
822 People Who Help Us, 1982.
Photography by Tim Clark.

Ladybird by Design

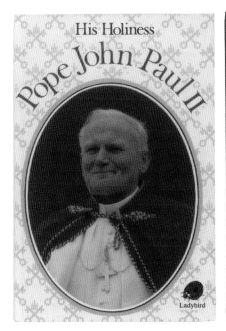 

His Holiness Pope John Paul II
816 Famous People, 1982.

H.M. Queen Elizabeth
The Queen Mother
816 Famous People, 1981.
Cover photography by Country
Life Books.

Once Ladybird had broken with tradition, the doors were open for other changes and in 1979 the publishers began to move away from illustration and to experiment with photography. The Hobbies and Interests titles (series 633) were reissued with a photographic redesign: *How to Make Wooden Toys* and *How to Make Puppets* were useful guides, but perhaps lacked the charm of their predecessors. Famous People (series 816) featured titles such as *H. M. The Queen*, *Pope John Paul II* and *H. M. Queen Elizabeth The Queen Mother*, in which the use of photography seemed appropriate. People Who Help Us (series 822) included titles such as *The Police Force*, *The Nurse*, *The Fire Service* and *The Postal Service*. These were interesting but very different in look to the 1960s series People at Work (series 606B).

A new precedent for Ladybird was set in August 1981 with the publication of *The Royal Wedding*. The photographic images from Charles and Diana's nuptials were vital and the production schedule tight – 500,000 copies of the book were available just four days after the event. The book, priced at 50p, sold very quickly, with sales soon exceeding 1.75 million copies; by the end of 1981 it had sold over 2 million copies.

Royal Wedding
First published 3 August 1981.
Cover photography by John Scott.

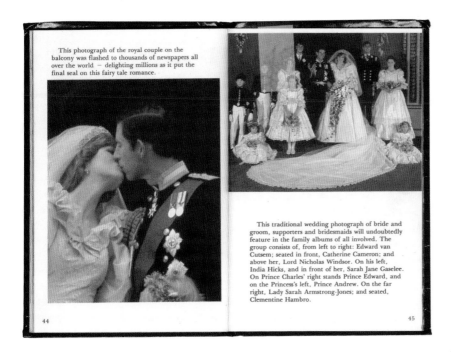

This photograph of the royal couple on the balcony was flashed to thousands of newspapers all over the world – delighting millions as it put the final seal on this fairy tale romance.

This traditional wedding photograph of bride and groom, supporters and bridesmaids will undoubtedly feature in the family albums of all involved. The group consists of, from left to right: Edward van Cutsem; seated in front, Catherine Cameron; and above her, Lord Nicholas Windsor. On his left, India Hicks, and in front of her, Sarah Jane Gaselee. On Prince Charles' right stands Prince Edward, and on the Princess's left, Prince Andrew. On the far right, Lady Sarah Armstrong-Jones; and seated, Clementine Hambro.

44

45

Royal Wedding
First published 3 August 1981.
Interior photography by John Scott.

The Royal Wedding

The production of *Royal Wedding* had been planned meticulously. Audrey Daly, the book's editor, met with John Scott, the royal photographer, in London on the eve of the wedding to discuss the images for the book. On the day of the event, Scott directed a further thirty photographers to ensure appropriate shots were available. Sixty photographs were chosen from the hundreds taken and the text for the book was written by Audrey on the journey back from London to Loughborough in time for a 5 a.m. production deadline. The text was then typeset using a computerized typesetting programme, photographs were processed at 6 a.m., and the book's first photographic plates were laid out at 7 a.m. Once the page proofs were checked, the presses started to print and, with the bindery working flat out, 10,000 copies were printed and bound per hour. It was an incredible feat – a marvel of design, editorial and production that ensured that Ladybird's book about the wedding of the century was published and in the shops in record time.

BOTH PAGES:
The Vanishing Monster
855 Puddle Lane, 1985.
Illustrations by
Mark Chadwick.

Ladybird

Reading
Programme
Stage 1

Puddle Lane

The vanishing monster

Sheila McCullagh

Davy sat very still.
He kept very quiet.
Soon, he saw a long green tail.

Davy saw
a long green tail.

14

15

Whilst Ladybird was branching out and starting to appeal to new audiences it was also keen not to lose its place as the publisher responsible for teaching children to read. With the Key Words Reading Scheme still going strong into its second decade, Ladybird also launched the Puddle Lane Reading Programme in January 1985. The initial series comprised twelve titles with more planned that would eventually take the series to over fifty books across five colour-coded reading stages. Puddle Lane was a relatively simple proposition – each book featured the text to be read by the parent or teacher on the left-hand page and on the right, beneath the illustration and in larger type, sat the key words from the story for the child to read and learn. It was described as the biggest book venture in twenty years. In October 1985 Yorkshire Television also began broadcasting a television series based on the books. This was a massive success and reprints of the books were under-taken. In the future, further book tie-ins with other television programmes would also mean big business for Ladybird.

Keen to exploit new formats, Ladybird next experimented with audio
cassettes, producing fiction and non-fiction book and cassette packages.
Ladybird also created jigsaw puzzles and games with other companies.
However, books linked to existing popular television series and films proved
the most successful venture and Ladybird moved increasingly to publish
these kinds of titles alongside their usual fare of fairy tales and reading
books. The Transformers and Masters of the Universe series may well
have appealed to young children of the mid-1980s but these US imports –
comic-book science fiction with little educational value – were a far cry from
Ladybird's beginnings. Whilst retaining Ladybird's high production values,
aesthetically these books took a new design direction. They often didn't
require the commissioning of illustrations at all, because stills from the TV
series could be used to illustrate the books instead.

However, the new direction that Ladybird's directors were taking the
company in was paying dividends – by 1985, Ladybird books were being
produced in sixty languages. In 1990, the annual Ladybird catalogue listed
over 600 titles, with new titles being published at the average rate of
100 per year.

Loughborough Past and Present

Despite its continued international success, Ladybird did not forget its origins. In 1988, Loughborough celebrated the centenary of its incorporation as a municipal borough and Ladybird joined in the celebrations. It published a special edition of the town's history with a print run of 10,000 copies – of which 4,000 were purchased by the town council.

Loughborough Past and Present
Centenary celebration edition, 1988.
Cover photography by Tim Clark.

Despite the recession of the early 1990s and the loss of some jobs at the company, Ladybird held steady, mainly due to increasing sales in Europe. Exports accounted for almost forty per cent of all sales and, in recognition, the company was rewarded with the British Printing Industries Export Achievement Award.

A new publishing deal was struck with Disney in 1991, and it was envisaged that both the 1992 opening of the Euro Disney Resort in Paris and Disney Stores in the UK would be financially beneficial for the company. This was a clear deviation from the usually overt British emphasis, with the company now appearing to embrace an all-American view of the world in a selection of their licensed titles. Creating popular products for the modern child was the motivation and the partnership with Disney enabled this; between mid-1991 and the end of 1992 Ladybird published 110 Disney titles with sales of 6.5 million books in total. *Beauty and the Beast* alone achieved sales of 500,000 copies. Disney sales continued upwards, reaching a staggering 20 million copies by 1995, with *The Lion King* film tie-in proving a particularly huge hit. Ladybird and Disney seemed like a perfect partnership.

In addition to the successful licensed character publishing programme, it was business as usual for Ladybird innovation, with the 1990s also heralding a first foray into board books for babies and toddlers, a relaunch into non-fiction for children aged six and over, and exploration of different types of formats, styling and illustration. Although the small hardback book was still dominant, Ladybird also began to expand its remit into paperbacks, activity books and novelty titles at different prices.

In 1997, two years after Ladybird became part of the Penguin Group, a special memorial book, *Diana, Princess of Wales*, was published following the death of Princess Diana. Hitting the book stands just ten days after her death, the book immediately took the number-two position in the UK hardback bestsellers list. As well as striking a chord with the depth of public feeling over the loss of Princess Diana, the success of the book was also assured by Ladybird's use of contemporary photography and its established back catalogue of titles centred on the Royal Family.

Ladybird by Design

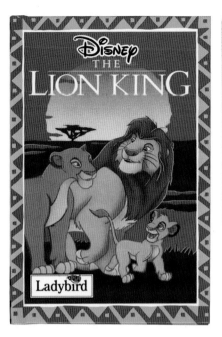

The Lion King
Book of the film, 1994.

Beauty and the Beast
Book of the film, 1992.

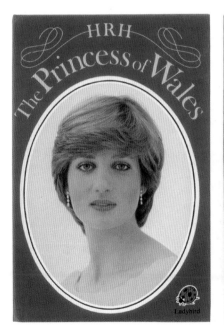

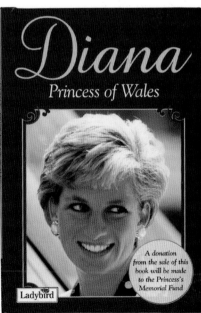

HRH The Princess of Wales
816 Famous People, 1982.

Diana Princess of Wales
1997. With photographs
by Tim Graham.

A is for Apple, 1992.
Illustrations by Lynn N. Grundy.

From Disney to Diana, fairy tales to foreign editions, Ladybird could do no wrong – it appeared that the company had the Midas touch. But by 1998, with Penguin beginning to assume overall management of the Ladybird business, there began a period of instability in Loughborough. In November of that year it was announced that the printing works would close, and with it 210 local jobs lost. This was a sad day for Loughborough, the spiritual home of Ladybird since Wills & Hepworth's formation in 1904. In April 1999, Ladybird produced a special edition of *Tootles the Taxi* that was presented to every member of staff working on the last day at the factory.

Special limited staff edition of *Tootles the Taxi*, showing a copy of the book in a slipcase and the numbered end-paper. A copy was presented to every member of staff on their last day at the Loughborough factory in 1999.

Following the closure of Ladybird's Loughborough site the publishing interests were divided into two lists. The Home Learning team was based in Nottingham and responsible for early learning, learning to read and baby and toddler titles. Popular Culture, based in London, was focused on creating new-style products aimed at children themselves as purchasers, with Disney and other character tie-ins essential aspects of this list.

In 2000, Ladybird began embracing new ways of reaching its audience. It was the first UK publishing company to provide a telephone helpline for its customers, giving parents advice on teaching children to read and on books for children. In the same year, Ladybird also launched its first website, a brave step at the dawn of the Internet era.

In 2005, the partnership with Disney came to an end. However, Ladybird continued unabated with the ongoing publication of high-quality early-learning titles and storybooks, and by capitalizing on other existing licences for the likes of Dreamworks, Warner Bros., Topsy and Tim, Angelina Ballerina and a brand-new character called Peppa Pig. Today, Peppa remains a runaway success for Ladybird. With total sales of books now in the millions, the popular pig also celebrated her tenth birthday in 2014.

Topsy and Tim also continues to be a best-selling brand for pre-school children. It has recently undergone a transformation with the twins appearing on BBC television channel CBeebies in a live-action format. The Ladybird team and Jean Adamson (the author of the Topsy and Tim titles) worked closely on ideas and scripts with the maker of the series, Darrall Macqueen. Penguin also invested in the production, which enabled Ladybird to go beyond the book and into live-action television production for the first time.

A Day at the Fair
Angelina Ballerina, 2002.
Angelina Ballerina © copyright
HIT Entertainment PLC.

The Snack Catcher
Scooby Doo, 2005.
Scooby Doo © copyright
Warner Bros. Entertainment Inc.

Lost Glasses
Peppa Pig, 2005.
Peppa Pig © copyright Astley
Baker Davis Ltd / Contender Ltd.

Hide and Seek
Peppa Pig, 2005.
Peppa Pig © copyright Astley
Baker Davis Ltd / Contender Ltd.

Hide and Seek
Peppa Pig, 2005.
Peppa Pig © copyright Astley
Baker Davis Ltd / Contender Ltd.

Ladybird by Design

Topsy and Tim's Birthday Party
1981. By Jean and Gareth Adamson.

*Topsy and Tim Have a
Birthday Party*
2003. By Jean and Gareth Adamson.

*Topsy and Tim Have a
Birthday Party*
2009. By Jean and Gareth Adamson.
Illustrations by Belinda Worsley.

Little Red Riding Hood
Ladybird Tales, 2012.
Illustrations by
Marina Le Ray.

The Gingerbread Man
Ladybird Tales, 2012.
Illustrations by
Daniel Howarth.

The Gingerbread Man
Ladybird Tales, 2012.
Illustrations by
Daniel Howarth.

The sly old fox swam a little further
out into the river.

Then he turned his head again and
said, "Little gingerbread boy, you
are too heavy for my back. You will
get wet. Jump onto my nose."

So the little gingerbread boy
jumped onto the fox's nose.

38

Ladybird by Design

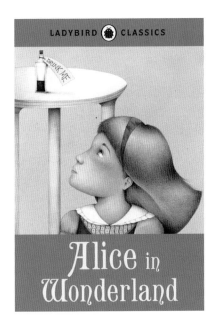

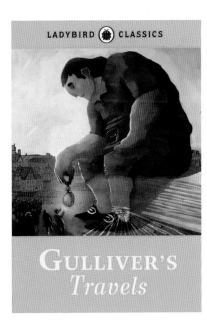

Alice in Wonderland
Ladybird Classics, 2012.
Illustrations by
Ester García-Cortés.

Gulliver's Travels
Ladybird Classics, 2012.
Illustrations by
Ciaran Duffy.

Ladybird's popularity continues today, with the publisher recognizing the value of its back catalogue, as well as continuing to develop carefully researched, innovative front-list publishing. The stories in the Ladybird Tales series, reissued in 2012, are based on Vera Southgate's original text for Well-loved Tales, continuing the legacy of Ladybird's focus on fairy tales. The Ladybird Classics series, also from 2012 and a reader's natural progression from Ladybird Tales, makes everyone's favourite stories accessible to young readers, with thoughtfully abridged retellings of classics such as *Alice in Wonderland*, *Gulliver's Travels* and *Peter Pan*.

Read it Yourself, originally launched in 1977, continues to the present day with almost a hundred titles available in its latest incarnation. The text and artwork remain carefully thought out and the books are designed to ensure the best possible experience for children learning to read, with the artwork working hard to give richness and detail to the simplified stories. The series has been brought up to date through the inclusion of both traditional fairy tales and licensed character stories, featuring Peppa Pig, Topsy and Tim and Peter Rabbit amongst others, and exists in print, ebook and app forms.

Little Red Riding Hood
Read it yourself
with Ladybird, 2013.
Illustrations by
Diana Mayo.

Alice in Wonderland
Read it yourself
with Ladybird, 2014.
Illustrations by
Barbara Bongini.

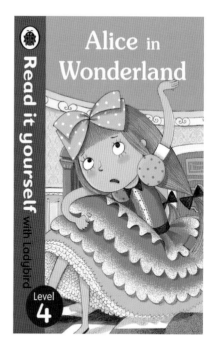

Alice in Wonderland
Read it yourself
with Ladybird, 2014.
Illustrations by
Barbara Bongini.

Ladybird by Design

The Key Words Reading Scheme remains the linchpin of Ladybird's international success and continues to be published, some half a century since first launching, in thirty-six territories worldwide, teaching literally millions of children to read. Lifetime sales of Key Words books are expected to reach 100 million copies by 2015, the year of Ladybird's anniverary.

Today, Ladybird's motto is 'for every age and every stage'. This is a mantra that the publishing company holds dear, committed as it is to nurturing children's development and supporting parents, carers and teachers. Ladybird ensures that it remains at the cutting edge of new advances in reading and education from birth onwards, as well as pushing the boundaries in innovative, high-quality art and design.

The bestselling series Baby Touch, for example, launched in 2005 and aimed at children from birth to two years old, has a bold, graphic look that entertains and stimulates young babies who are only able to differentiate very high-contrast colours during their first few months. Much imitated but never bettered, the series has been translated into twenty different languages and has international lifetime sales of over 5 million copies.

Tummy Time
Baby Touch, 2014.

Baby Touch: Peekaboo!
App, 2011.

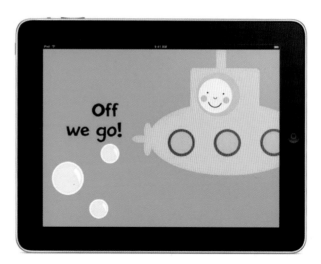

Baby Touch: Happy Babies
App, 2012.

Ladybird I'm Ready to Spell
App, 2014.

Ladybird by Design

Ladybird is also now an innovator in digital publishing through its interactive apps and ebooks, and aims to guide children through important learning milestones and support them at every stage of their development across all digital platforms as well as print books.

A century old in 2015, Ladybird retains both its prominent position as one of the UK's foremost children's book publishers and its almost unprecedented brand-name awareness amongst consumers. By continuing to embrace new mediums – from the telephone helpline and early website launch to film tie-ins and television shows, and from a strong presence on social media to digital ebooks and apps – Ladybird has remained relevant to its audience at every point.

'For every age and every stage' is certainly an apt description for the publisher best-known for having created books adored by children and trusted by parents and teachers for generations. The backstory of this amazing British publishing success story is the excellent editorial, design and production decisions made by a committed and passionate company, which has stayed dedicated to its audience throughout its 100-year history.

Penguin, Ladybird's parent company, merged with Random House in July 2013 to form Penguin Random House, the world's first truly global trade publishing group, and Ladybird is now part of its children's division. Penguin Random House is a company with a unique history and world-wide appeal that ensures Ladybird a safe home for many years to come. Long live Ladybird.

www.ladybird.com
www.vintageladybird.com

Index

Figures in *italics* indicate illustrations. Figures in **bold** indicate main textual references to individual illustrators. Series and individual titles are indexed only if they are mentioned in the main text.

A note on Ladybird series numbers

The first two digits of a series number indicate the year in which the first book in the series was printed. The third number is thought to designate the month the first book was initially released, as Ladybird would normally only publish books from January–September.

Picture credits

Unless otherwise stated below, all images have been scanned from original books and artwork held in the Ladybird archive at the University of Reading or from Ladybird's own collection, with copyright © Ladybird Books Ltd.

p2 photograph copyright © Leicestershire County Council Museum Service; pp12–13 photograph copyright © Douglas Keen family archive; p14 top left photograph from The Definitive Guide to Ladybird Books copyright © The Wee Web; p14 bottom left photograph copyright © Leicestershire, Leicester and Rutland Record Office; p16 copyright © The British Library Board, WP. 9629/9 (front cover); p17 centre right copyright © The British Library Board, WP. 9629/10 (Plate of thumb); p17 top copyright © The British Library Board, WP. 9629/10 (front cover); p24 centre left M. McNeill/Stringer/ Hulton Archive/Getty Images; p24 top left The National Archives/SSPL/Getty Images; p24 bottom left photograph copyright © Douglas Keen family archive; p30 photograph copyright © Douglas Keen family archive; p31 bottom right photograph copyright © Douglas Keen family archive; p31 top right and centre right photograph from The Definitive Guide to Ladybird Books copyright © The Wee Web by kind permission of John Muschialli; pp32–42 all photographs copyright © Douglas Keen family archive; pp56–57 all photographs copyright © Douglas Keen family archive; p64 top left © Bettmann/Corbis; p84 top left photograph copyright © Tony Murray and Lorna Hillman; p112 centre courtesy of Helen Day, www.ladybirdflyawayhome.com; p207 top left photograph copyright © family of Bernard Robinson; p207 top centre photograph copyright © Estate of Charles Tunnicliffe; p207 top right photograph copyright © family of Robert Ayton; p207 centre left photograph copyright © family of John Kenney; p207 centre middle photograph courtesy of Helen Day, www.ladybirdflyawayhome.com; p207 centre right photograph copyright © Helen Day, www.ladybirdflyawayhome.com; p207 bottom left photograph copyright © Douglas Keen family archive; p207 bottom centre photograph copyright © Douglas Keen family archive; p221 all images courtesy of Helen Day, www.ladybirdflyawayhome.com; p243 all images courtesy of Stefan Davey.

Every effort has been made to trace copyright holders and to obtain their permission for the use of copyright material. The publisher apologizes for any errors or omissions and would be grateful if notified of any corrections that should be incorporated in future reprints or editions of this book.

Acknowledgements

Firstly, big thanks go to my mother, Ann Lee, for introducing me to my first Ladybird books as a child – I had quite a collection compiled during the mid-late 1960s and through the 1970s. Secondly, I'd like to thank the staff in the numerous charity shops across London and the South East who helped me to rebuild my long-lost collection as research for this book.

Guy Baxter at the wonderful Ladybird Archive at Reading University allowed me to open box after box of beautiful Ladybird artwork and then patiently listened to me gush in awe at the quality of the work as each piece was revealed. Caroline Alexander and Jenny Pearce, Douglas Keen's daughters, gave me an extra-special insight into their father's life and times at Ladybird, as did William Murray's children Tony Murray and Lorna Hillman. Helen Day from www.ladybirdflyawayhome.com was a fount of useful information and resources.

At Ladybird I'd like to thank Publisher Heather Crossley and her remarkable team – Nicola Bird, Isobel Booth, Ronnie Fairweather, Sara Glenn, and Art Director Jo Garden – thank you so much for your support, encouragement and cajoling. Huge thanks also to the book's editor Emma Marriott and designer Tom Sanderson; great teamwork!

At London College of Communication my thanks go to my staff team in the School of Design for allowing me the space and time to research and write and to Alice Clark and Nina Crane for compiling lists of Ladybird books I'd found and those I was still on the hunt for.

My final thanks, and all my love, to my family; my sons Louie, Jake and Felix Zeegen for their support and Rebecca Wright for having the faith and for allowing me to stockpile the Ladybird books she often accompanied me in my search for.

Lawrence Zeegen